"A thoroughly researched, courageous critique of organizational practices on women and human flourishing. A must-read for women in Christian organizations."
Mimi Haddad, president of CBE International

"While many leaders of missional organizations no doubt want their organizations to be places of flourishing for both women and men, how to intentionally enable this is not always clear. Help is at hand! Birmingham and Sallinen Simard, in bringing us their belonging culture framework, detail six areas that, taken together, demystify what such a place of flourishing might look like and how to lead into it. Richly illustrated with research findings, stories, indicators, and examples, *Creating Cultures of Belonging* is essential reading for leaders seeking to transform their organizations in this important area."
Deborah Hancox, international coordinator, Micah Global

"The collective wisdom and practical guidance that these experienced women bring will be a gift to your organizations. As a Latina pastor, activist, neighbor, and mother, I wish there were more institutions that were intentional about keeping talent."
Sandra Maria Van Opstal, executive director of Chasing Justice and author of *The Next Worship*

"This work of research and personal insight has the power to help Christians build inclusive work cultures where everyone belongs and everyone thrives. Throughout this book, Birmingham and Sallinen Simard shine a light on where organizational faith leaders have missed the mark and how they can correct course. This is an important paradigm-shifting book that can transform not just organizations but readers."
Karen Gonzalez, human resources director at World Relief and author of *The God Who Sees*

"In *Creating Cultures of Belonging*, the authors begin by calling out the institutionalized misogyny that too often oppresses women in our organizational contexts. Then they articulate a comprehensive and compelling blueprint for organizational transformation—one that engages every aspect of organizational life, including theology, leadership, policy, culture, and more. If you long to see your organization become a place where both women and men can truly belong, this is the book for you."
Rob Dixon, author of *Together in Ministry*

"This is an absolute must-read for men and women in leadership. As I lead a global organization, I take pride in the stereotypes my organization has broken. However, the contrast that exists outside this space is not invisible either. The chapter on how most missional organizations have a problem with women was gripping and affirming. The richness of the experience both authors bring to every single chapter is not just evident but also points the reader to introspection. I've oftentimes been referred to as the ambitious, overconfident woman in the workplace, and this book has helped me find peace with being unique, different, and misunderstood."
Anu George Canjanathoppil, CEO of International Justice Mission Canada

"Writing in a candid, collaborative, mutually amplifying style that exemplifies the very leadership they commend, Beth Birmingham and Eeva Sallinen Simard offer a book that is desperately needed. In turns both challenging and empowering, it is not only a compelling argument for shared egalitarian leadership in mission agencies but also research-based, theologically grounded, systemic instruction for equipping leaders who default to exclusionary models they have previously seen and in which they have been trained. This is a guidebook to a healthier, more God-honoring way of creating an increasingly effective and flourishing organizational culture. I will be recommending it for my clients, requiring it for my students, and rereading it myself."

Tod Bolsinger, executive director of the Church Leadership Institute and author of *Tempered Resilience: How Leaders Are Formed in the Crucible of Change*

"Whether churches, nonprofits, or corporations, our organizations are deprived of their full potential when we fail to recognize the richness and value of diverse perspectives in God's kingdom. Beth Birmingham and Eeva Sallinen Simard awaken us to the perils of structural sameness and invite us to embrace new possibilities of welcoming and valuing every voice. *Creating Cultures of Belonging* is for anyone seeking to build a missional community marked by mutuality and respect."

Peter Greer, president of HOPE International and author of *The Gift of Disillusionment*

"How I wish this book had been available to me decades ago when I began leading at a table filled only with men! Any culture that seeks to be truly inclusive will benefit from taking a deep dive into these pages. Here you will find thoughtful research, practical steps, and real-life stories that inspire both men and women to do better as we seek to serve God's kingdom as brothers and sisters. We can and must do better. This book will help!"

Nancy Beach, leadership coach and coauthor with Samantha Beach Kiley of *Next Sunday*

CREATING CULTURES OF BELONGING

CULTIVATING ORGANIZATIONS
WHERE WOMEN AND MEN THRIVE

BETH BIRMINGHAM
EEVA SALLINEN SIMARD

FOREWORDS BY MYAL GREENE
AND EMILY SARMIENTO

An imprint of InterVarsity Press
Downers Grove, Illinois

InterVarsity Press
P.O. Box 1400 | Downers Grove, IL 60515-1426
ivpress.com | email@ivpress.com

InterVarsity Press® is the publishing division of InterVarsity Christian Fellowship/USA®. For more information, visit intervarsity.org.

Scripture quotations, unless otherwise noted, are from the Common English Bible, copyright © 2011. Used by permission. All rights reserved.

While any stories in this book are true, some names and identifying information may have been changed to protect the privacy of individuals.

The publisher cannot verify the accuracy or functionality of website URLs used in this book beyond the date of publication.

Cover design and image composite: David Fassett
Interior design: Daniel van Loon

ISBN 978-0-8308-3916-2 (print) | ISBN 978-0-8308-3917-9 (digital)

Printed in the United States of America ∞

Library of Congress Cataloging-in-Publication Data
A catalog record for this book is available from the Library of Congress.

29 28 27 26 25 24 23 22 | 15 14 13 12 11 10 9 8 7 6 5 4 3 2 1

TO THE WOMEN

who have been excluded

TO THE MEN

who are allies

FOR THE CULTURE OF BELONGING

we can create together

CONTENTS

Foreword by Myal Greene   *1*

Foreword by Emily Sarmiento   3

Introduction   5

1 The Missional Organization Has a Problem with Women   9

2 A Culture of Belonging   24

3 *Imago Dei*—Addressing Theology   42

4 A Clear Case   52

5 A Reclaimed Organizational Culture   64

6 Human Resources for Cultures of Belonging   83

7 Developing People for Cultures of Belonging   103

8 The Leadership Will to Make a Change   119

9 Women and Men Beyond the Workplace   134

Conclusion   153

Acknowledgments   163

The Belonging Culture Framework Summary   164

Suggested Reading   167

Notes   171

FOREWORD

MYAL GREENE

f you are holding this book, you have likely seen how gender inequality can harm missional organizations and wonder how you can foster change. You may be concerned that Christian organizations seem decades behind secular organizations in addressing these issues. You might also be struggling with why your organization has so many female employees but few women in leadership. Like you, I have wrestled with these questions, and I'm encouraged that you are reading this book.

Across just about every organizational setting, women face challenges in the workplace that men don't. Yet in Christian organizations, progress toward change has been slow. It would be naive or dishonest to claim that being a man hasn't benefited me in my professional development. For example, throughout my career in vocational Christian ministry, all my supervisors have been men. As a male leader in a Christian nonprofit, competency in creating a culture of belonging for both women and men is often considered an optional skill. Yet women must learn to navigate bias and inequitable systems daily. As leaders, we must recognize this dynamic and make meaningful changes.

Beth Birmingham and Eeva Sallinen Simard have been two of my most trusted guides in my journey to understand these issues and lead better. Eeva and I have worked together at World Relief for a decade. As a leader, she is skilled at drawing out the strengths of everyone on her team and helping those teams be successful as they complement each other's gifts. As a change agent, she has been instrumental in helping design a global initiative to help our international offices make meaningful steps toward gender equality. In the classrooms of Eastern University's graduate programs, Beth has helped shape my understanding of building healthy organizational cultures, and as a consultant to World Relief, she has helped train teams I've led to grow, flourish, and see the strengths in one another. They are trusted collaborators who have helped challenge and equip me to create leadership environments where both women and men can flourish. But most importantly, they are always ready to help me learn from my mistakes with candor and grace.

Christian organizations have a problem with how we handle gender-related issues, and Beth and Eeva speak with firsthand experiences. Although a harsh critique could be justified in this book, they navigate the subject by expressing love for the organizations they serve and a hopeful vision of the future. They make their case with a blend of empirical data and personal experiences. All of it reinforces a valuable lesson I have learned along the way. When we build more inclusive, equitable organizations, we unlock new skills from every team member and multiply our talents. If God has called your organization to proclaim the gospel, serve vulnerable communities, or any other world-changing mission, you must consider how your organization's culture impacts your ministry.

Although I have spent hours with Eeva and Beth discussing these issues over the years, reading this book has inspired me with fresh insights. I hope this book is equally powerful in your hands.

While this is a book for men and women alike, I hope and pray it ends up in the hands of many male leaders—not just those ready to make a change but the skeptics too. I believe what is on the subsequent pages has the potential to transform your organization and many others. If we learn to understand the root problems that cause gender inequity in the Christian workplace, set aside our own biases, and use the proven methods described in this book, we will have endless opportunities to make a kingdom impact for the glory of God. But if we fail to get it right, we will continue to repeat the mistakes of the past that have routinely made the Christian workplace inequitable for women and stifled the overall impact of our ministry. The stakes are high! How will you respond?

FOREWORD

EMILY SARMIENTO

I knew by university I would serve God in leadership of global social sector work. My career started in secular development, where I thought anything was possible. Female leaders were not uncommon. I carefully studied Jo Luck, then CEO at Heifer International, my first NGO. "HeadHeifer" was my career vision and my laptop password because I believed I could do what Jo Luck did.

Fast-forward some years, and I found myself in the US Christian relief and development sector. To get in, I took professional steps backward to a coordinator role, where I was often reduced to a secretary by men four decades older. I progressed into new environments where a male colleague told me to go home and have children. Other men facilitated male networking activities and men-only trips where alliances were built and strategies set. Toxic work behaviors compounded my doubts about whether I could be a successful leader, wife, and mom. I questioned if I even wanted to lead within some of the organizational cultures I witnessed.

When I started, there were few to no women in significant leadership roles in the faith-based organizations around me. I remember how I celebrated the first visible naming of a female CEO in our space. Now, at this writing, women hold 13 percent of first-chair roles within the organizations of our trade association . . . *a decade later.*

I share this to note two observations. These stem from my own experiences, data I've consumed, and lived experiences shared by other women within US-headquartered missional organizations.

First, faith-based organizations are often complicit in dimming the full reflection of God's image within the workforce. It is frequently the secular organizations—not Christian—where more is done to promote, support, and celebrate women in leadership.

Second, patriarchy is strongest in faith-based circles—including NGOs—though Jesus centered and elevated women throughout his ministry on earth. Broken theology cascades from church culture to missional organizations who then tend to export it to the contexts in which they serve.

Practically, this means many Christian NGOs may preach and fundraise off anti-exploitation or equal access to education but not invest in equitable practice or equal access to exec teams and boardrooms. This points to an integrity crisis in pockets of the sector.

Christ-followers are called to pursue shalom—peace, wholeness, and completeness in the world. Justice is the restorative work of creating the conditions for shalom to exist.

I applaud Beth and Eeva for their thoughtful research and careful road map toward shalom on this topic, the vision for gender justice in the faith-based missional sector. It's not a quick fix or one-dimensional formula. Rather, they have articulated well the organizational *system* needed for women and men to flourish together in missional calling.

While the road is long and the work is hard, the effort is worthwhile and in fact essential. Our sector's pursuit of shalom for others will have greater integrity, and impact will accelerate when shalom manifests in our organizational cultures.

INTRODUCTION

On a beautiful afternoon on Lake Malawi, during a leadership training retreat, we've split the women and men into two separate groups. This is a learned custom from church, where we're used to seeing "ladies' tea" and "men's fellowship breakfast" in the weekly bulletin. Being in separate groups underlines the distinct roles and responsibilities women and men have carried in ministry. Men have led; women have served. Men have strategized; women have nurtured. This division has not served our institutions well, but today it provides a familiar space for truth-telling and private matters, topics intended only for sharing with peers.

The women sit scattered on couches or cross-legged on the floor holding cups of tea or coffee, and they share from the heart. In certain cultures and groups this comes easier than others, but by the end of our time together we'll have reached some deeper topics. Across the grounds, the men are engaging in a corresponding activity.

When we reconvene with the male trainer on our team, we discover we've been having two different but very similar conversations.

In both rooms leaders have expressed deep concern for the health and success of their organizations. They hope for a better balance between their demanding work and family and personal well-being. The worries, prayers, aspirations, and fears aren't gender-specific. The women don't worry more about their families and less about funding cuts or global trends affecting their programming. In fact, statistically, the women will have worked twice as hard to get to the seat they serve in and are more than qualified for leadership. They are not less informed or too emotional for strategic conversations but are well-suited for their roles, and they have decades of experience to contribute to the problems at hand.

Despite positive experiences such as the one with this team on Lake Malawi, at the end of the day, women are still missing in organizational leadership.

This is because many still hold to a wrongful and outdated belief that men are better suited to lead. That women are too emotional, too gentle and kind to make hard decisions. That men are more decisive, objective, and natural leaders altogether. That a woman's voice is harder to hear or needs translation, while a man speaks at a pitch that commands attention and order. That there are not enough seats at the table to accommodate both women and men.

We urgently need to create diversity of women and men leading together. The problems we face—a global pandemic, climate shifts, racial and cultural reckoning, wars—are too great for homogenous groups to solve. The world is bursting at the seams, and without diverse voices seated around our tables, we are far from even naming the problems we need to solve. We need new eyes, new hands—new ways of looking at and solving old problems and future unknowns.

You may nod your head at these ideas and agree wholeheartedly. Your organization or community may even have attempted to do the work to become more diverse—but failed to move the needle. There was that difficult senior woman who didn't quite work out. There was that young leader you hired who failed to be assertive and strategic enough. The composition of the board hasn't gone above 20 percent nonwhite-male since the founding of the organization, and because of stakeholder expectations and archaic leadership models, you feel light years away from considering a woman for the top job of CEO.

Equality of women and men often falls into the "important but not urgent" category as an organizational goal. This is at least a step up from "unfortunate necessity," where it spent most of the last several decades.

Change is on the horizon, however. Based on our experiences in the non-profit space among what we call *missional organizations* in this book, prospective staff and leaders, board members, and donors now routinely inquire about gender inclusion statistics when considering how to support an organization—not just in program design and implementation but also in the composition of work and leadership teams. In the next decades, organizations that want to compete for the most critical and talented workforce are the ones prepared to take decisive action to create a more diverse workplace community.

Organizations and leaders who haven't found a way to pursue greater diversity will find themselves lagging behind in the most important global trend in the nonprofit sector—inclusive development and the inclusive leadership it will require.

* * *

This book is a love letter to faith-based organizations and all who want to see their organizations improve for the sake of those we serve, as well as for the sake of those serving—the staff and leaders of these organizations.

We love this sector enough to celebrate its strengths, and we love it enough to challenge it in its blind spots, in its preference for patriarchal leadership models, in its burnout pace, in its tendency to go after shiny new things rather than stay the course on the road toward belonging. The sector can no longer afford this: creating cultures where everyone brings their best and feels they belong will result in better performance outcomes and radically new insights, whether the sphere is housing, child development, community development, water quality, public health, microenterprise, or any of the many other areas our organizations serve.

This book is for every reader who wants to see greater equality between women and men lived out in our organizational communities. As we embark on this journey with you, we assume you share our view that women are well-suited for leadership, just as men are. You believe that women are gifted, talented, creative, and righteously ambitious, created by God to work alongside men in any role or at any level of leadership.

If your theology brings to you a place where you believe women should play limited, complementary roles to men, this book isn't for you.

• • •

Expanding donor pools and dollars. Innovation that leads to better programming. A larger geographic footprint. These are all significant blessings our organizations can experience.

But we believe that many of us are being held back from experiencing the greatest blessing God has intended. As the psalmist writes:

> How wonderful, how beautiful,
>   when brothers and sisters get along!
> It's like costly anointing oil
>   flowing down head and beard,
> Flowing down Aaron's beard,
>   flowing down the collar of his priestly robes.
> It's like the dew on Mount Hermon
>   flowing down the slopes of Zion.
> Yes, that's where GOD commands the blessing,
>   ordains eternal life. (Psalm 133:1-3 *The Message*)

Our organizations haven't even begun to touch the blessing described in these verses.

Isn't it time we did?

CHAPTER ONE

THE MISSIONAL ORGANIZATION
HAS A PROBLEM WITH WOMEN

The executive team sat in a conference room answering the question, "Who are our next generation of leaders?" This leadership-pipeline conversation was the right one, the responsible one, even with transitions several years away. The name of a female midlevel leader flashed on the screen.

"Not her," said her supervisor, a male senior vice president, known for routinely pulling sixty-plus-hour workweeks despite having school-age kids at home. "She's made it known that with kids and her husband's demanding job, she doesn't have the bandwidth to lead right now."

A female executive there knew exactly why this woman would have said that: she didn't want to lead like her boss. So she hesitantly interjected, "Maybe she just doesn't know what being a leader could mean for *her*."

In an average organization, this next-generation female leader would statistically have few leadership role models. In the movement to elevate more women into leadership, this phenomenon is described as, "You can't be what you can't see." Left to consider whether she could lead like her male boss—maintaining his schedule, mirroring his temperament, carrying on his relentless dedication to work despite obligations at home or in other areas of interest—she is forced to answer with an unequivocal "no." Without better and more inclusive examples of what being a leader could look like, many women don't see a pathway to leadership for themselves.

The bottom line is, there aren't enough women in leadership roles to demonstrate what it looks like when women lead, let alone a critical mass of women who could truly make an impact and create a new leadership culture altogether.

In some contexts, women have carved out an occasional role among majority male or men-only leadership teams. For years we have observed that women succeed and are celebrated in leadership when they demonstrate a male-like leadership style—straight-shooting, confident, always on. We've also seen women who are admonished for these same qualities, told they are too aggressive and too confident, so they resort to making sure they are perceived as nice and easy to get along with. By midcareer, aspiring female leaders know that to succeed, they must leave their personalities and personal lives at the door and navigate a labyrinth of conflicting expectations.

Putting pressure on women to show up like men is a lose-lose outcome. Women lose a seat and their genuine voice at the table where important decisions are made. Men and women together lose the opportunity to learn from a shared, more balanced leadership model and the healthy culture it would mean for our organizations, communities, and homes.

EEVA'S STORY

Like most women, I (Eeva) have learned the hard way what it means to speak with my genuine voice. Growing up in a fundamentalist church, as the oldest of four sisters, I intentionally ignored the muted roles women played in that world. It wasn't until I began to toggle between motherhood, career, and leadership that I was forced to face how my patriarchal church community offered me no examples of women in leadership. Neither did it present opportunities for mentorship on how I could manage my many responsibilities. Despite my egalitarian marriage, the realities that faced me as a woman ended up changing how I experienced my Christian faith. Leaving my church after thirty years broke my heart, but I knew that to express the gift of leadership God had given me, I could not call "home" a community that was most comfortable if I kept silent.

I also should have known better, because I grew up in one of the most gender-equal countries in the world: Finland. As a young woman I had seen a number of close relatives and friends pursue motherhood and careers, leaning on the unparalleled support systems of yearlong maternity leave, daycare, long holidays, and respect for a division between work and the rest of life. When I entered working life in the United States I realized how flawed the system truly was, and my experience was exacerbated by the often-misogynistic attitudes of my church community. While my peers at home had support and affirmation as they entered motherhood, I was focused solely on not causing financial loss to my employer when I did the same. The contrast between the lives of my peers in Finland and my own reality was shocking.

I came to care about healthy leadership because of this contrast.

My yearbook picture, had I had one, wouldn't have described me as "most ambitious" but rather as "most friendly" or "most diplomatic." Creating spaces of cohesion and collaboration is my natural way of being. Because I had been silenced as a woman, it took me many years to realize that my "female" style is exactly what many teams need, and I began lean into it. It is my unique contribution to teams often composed of world-class technical experts, whether in the nonprofit sector or academia. Instead of shrinking this part of me, I have learned to use it as my superpower.

I've made my greatest impact on teams I've worked on and led by re-sourcing people to do their best work. I focus on the well-being of people because I believe it drives them to perform at their highest level and leads to the best results for the team as a whole. I believe good, healthy leadership that emphasizes every team member's well-being and personal strengths is not only possible but attainable. I also believe that this emphasis is the secret to unlocking gender equality in our organizations.

BETH'S STORY

I (Beth) was raised in a home where my parents held traditional roles. My dad was the breadwinner, while my mother, who contributed to the family income through Tupperware parties, was the caregiver and also the primary decision maker on finances and family matters. As a young girl I saw women teach at my Episcopal church and never gave a thought to gender roles growing up. When I was in my twenties I joined a church with superior egalitarian Bible teaching, and soon after I joined a Christian university's leadership center, which was led by three diverse individuals who modeled what they taught. Two were men; one was a woman. This was my introduction to a culture of belonging. The healthy leadership and organizational behaviors I espouse today can be attributed to the lessons I learned from them.

When I joined this university, it was filled with egalitarian theologians and led by a female president—the first woman to head a Protestant college in the United States. While some called her "hell on heels" for her masculine leadership style, I remember thinking I could see the flecks of glass in her hair from crashing her way through the glass ceiling. Undoubtedly her experience in a man's world such as academia formed some of her leadership style. Today we've learned to identify and call out the harsh critiques leveled against women who show up with leadership traits usually associated with men.

I was encircled by men and women who encouraged me to use my gifts for significant purposes. In my leadership role in the university's small leadership center that evolved into the school of leadership and development, I encountered the stark realities women and girls face in less egalitarian countries. When I traveled, too many meeting rooms I entered were filled with all men. Too many times I held a dear African sister as she wrestled with her family calling her selfish for using money to further her own education rather than paying for the education of relatives. Too many qualified female graduates from my program were never considered for top posts, despite their skills and qualifications.

I learned what cultural and systemic inequality looks like.

In 2015, the university where I served decided to refocus its programs nationally. I knew my calling to equip leaders in the most difficult places had not changed, so after twenty-two years of service, I surprised many when I left my tenured faculty position. It was in the international world of nongovernmental organizations (NGOs) that I confronted a second stark reality, but this time not on foreign soil. I came to realize that the systemic treatment of women as "second-class" is prevalent in faith-based organizations, particularly in their Western headquarters.

These experiences, the good and the less good, are what fueled our passion to write this book. Because we have known what a culture of belonging feels like, and what a difference it makes for staff success and everyday experience, we want women *and* men in the missional sector to feel it too.

THE MISSIONAL ORGANIZATION

In this book we talk about missional organizations.

We use this term as a catch-all to describe organizations united by faith-based or religious roots, including nonprofits, parachurch ministries, mission organizations, churches, conferences, educational institutions, and even some for-profits. The term *missional* is a bit of a buzzword with no real dictionary definition; we use it here to assume an organizational motivation that is centered on Christian faith. Missional organizations follow the example of Jesus, who sent out his disciples into "all the world." Throughout their histories, missional organizations have felt a strong prompting by faith to be sent out, whether in fighting poverty, serving refugees and displaced people, educating, advocating, creating microbusiness opportunities, or in the many capacities they serve people in our neighborhoods or around the world.

The missional sector uses the terms such as *integral mission* or *transformational development* to describe the coming together of "word and deed." René Padilla was among the first to challenge the patriarchal and Western-focused way of thinking about mission and development. He spoke of integral mission as the church, wherever it is located, being committed to communicating the gospel through everything it is, says, and does. Gil Odendaal, a leading teacher and expert on integral mission, often says, "Mixing word and deed is like mixing tea and milk: the two become inseparable. You can no longer tell them apart." In the missional organization, word and deed have become integrated, an inseparable part of our organizational DNA.

This approach gives missional organizations a special flavor; it is the unique handprint by which we do our work. But it does not come without challenges.

The global context of the missional organization forces us to continuously reevaluate this integral view of our work. Government funds cannot support explicitly religious programming. Many millennial staff don't feel comfortable being labeled as "faith-based" and are even less so being called "evangelical," not least because of the unwelcoming stigma these terms carry. Organizations work in geographic contexts that do not welcome a faith-based approach, which can even endanger the staff. Many organizations that were established on Christian or religious foundations no longer self-identify as faith-based, claim any religious affiliation, ask their staff to sign statements of faith, or require participation in weekly practices of devotion or prayer.

Despite these barriers, the faith-based actors in international and US-based programming continue to grow their footprint among nonprofits.

According to the United Nations Economic and Social Council estimate, faith-based organizations make up approximately 14 percent of NGOs globally. Christian organizations make up nearly 60 percent of that number. In the United States, of the more than 1.5 million registered nonprofits, religion-related organizations make up nearly 7 percent. According to GuideStar, there are 143,350 religious nonprofits in the United States, with over half of this number made up of Christian churches. Since some non-profits register as churches, and many churches do the work of nonprofits, the waters of an accurate count are muddied even further.

According to Katherine Marshall, who calls these organizations "faith-inspired," their footprint has steadily increased in the United Nations registry:

> Through the 1980s, the secular world, whether US or other foreign governments or UN agencies, took very little explicit notice of religious organizations. September 11 put a spotlight on religion and the culture wars at large, sadly generally in negative ways. Overall, however, today religion and religiously inspired work are much more on different agendas, but the priority of these organizations or their centrality to the development agendas varies from one administration or global leader to the next. Success in securing mainstream funding is often contingent on a capacity to cut across very different worldviews from their own.

Despite the enlarged footprint of faith-based nonprofits, their ability to secure continued support depends on their ability to communicate their mission not only to faith-aligned audiences but beyond. To reach across ideologies and to qualify for governmental and global funding, organizations are forced to continually reexamine what role faith, and especially the expression of faith, plays in their programmatic activities and interventions.

Some missional organizations are doing the hard work of shedding harmful ideologies and practices in their programming. Challenged by books such as *The White Man's Burden* and *When Helping Hurts*, as well as documentaries such as *Poverty, Inc.*, they are applying a different critical lens to their own sector. The historical "White savior" mentality is being challenged to give way to locally driven planning and leadership, where outside resources are welcomed only after the local community establishes priorities and needs and draws first on its own skills and resources. This approach requires the missional organization to enter as a guest and function as a servant. This is not a posture that comes easily when organizational goals, donor expectations, and money are driving the agenda.

The way organizations have "done development" in past decades is certainly open to examination and criticism. Part of this examination involves a rejection of terms such as *international development* and certainly *undeveloped world,* as well as dismantling the distorted image of donors and aid workers as heroic saviors, something the sector has held on to for far too long. Change is difficult, but a brave few organizations are forging the right path.

MISSIONAL ORGANIZATIONS AND THE PROBLEM WITH WOMEN

Change is also desperately needed in how missional organizations engage with women.

It might be easy to assume that missional organizations should hold the welcoming and belonging of everyone as central to the organizational culture. After all, if Jesus is at the center, shouldn't we, by his example, also welcome all?

The reality is that many organizations still carry the baggage of decades past. Their viewpoints have been formulated by their history and traditional theology, resulting in an organizational culture that is unwelcoming to women.

Over the decades the sector has not only struggled to create cultures that welcome all but has held on to unique historical and theological barriers. The theological views that still dominate in organizations have been gleaned from unchallenged denominational interpretations and practices. Histories are often intertwined with military, church, and missionary cultures, in which many household-name missional organizations have their roots. Unexamined, obsolete, and harmful cultures that center one-size-fits-all leadership still permeate many organizations, whether secular or missional. All these factors create a perfect storm in missional organizations, one that has long prevented the conversation around women's equality from even getting started.

Despite individual organizations' undertaking efforts to reexamine and reevaluate other harmful practices, the issue of women's unequal role lingers. Women's participation in leadership and decision making, along with their ability to shape the future of organizations, remains stunted. Organizations make decisions about forward motion in a complex world while still holding on to legacy policies, practices, and leadership styles that do not favor and even completely disregard women.

Jane, a participant in a focus group we conducted, states,

> During my tenure with my organization I've seen ten women enter and exit our executive team. They'll come in and make progress for six to eighteen months, and then suddenly something happens and they're out. Maybe it's that they can't do the job, sure, but the men don't have the same track record. Men serve in their roles for a decade at a time. Why is it that women are so unsuitable for these roles? What is holding women back? It's almost like some invisible qualifier cuts women out before they even get started.

The data confirms the same. Women make up more than 70 percent of the nonprofit workforce, including the secular sector, but just over 20 percent of the larger agencies have women as CEOs. A Gordon College study led by professors Amy Reynolds and Janel Curry assessed evangelical nonprofits' female leadership status in 2016 and found this segment dramatically lagging behind the general sector statistics. In the faith-based space, women lead just 2 percent of nonprofits larger than $10 million, and whereas larger secular nonprofit boards are led by 40 percent women, for faith-based organizations that statistic is well under 20 percent (see fig. 1). Consider these additional findings:

- Between 50 and 80 percent of the clients of services or programs of missional organization work are women and girls.
- More than 70 percent of the staff who serve in missional organizations are women.
- More than 50 percent of the people making donor decisions are women, even if their name isn't on the credit card or check.
- Women represent just over 2 percent of large missional organization CEOs and just over 20 percent of small to midsize organizations.

Why are women not making progress in the missional sector?

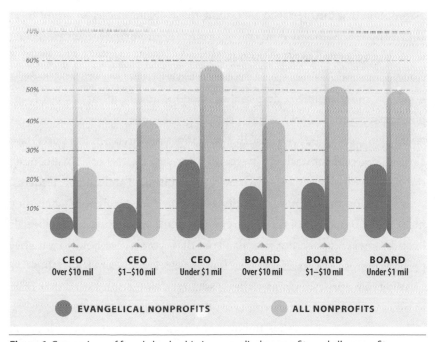

Figure 1. Comparison of female leadership in evangelical nonprofits and all nonprofits

Despite numerous examples of excellent female leaders, people tend to prioritize and gravitate toward male leadership, almost as a reflex. A recent analysis found that women are devalued in leadership positions when they occupy male-dominated roles and when they are evaluated by men. Men still struggle to see women as leaders, and the most conservative worldview downright believes that women are not created or wired for leadership.

There is a false belief that men are simply better at leadership and have more natural disposition for it. And who can blame most of us for believing this? We learn this from a very early age from the cultural context and familial practices we are raised in, and as people of faith we also learn it from the examples and teaching we receive at church. No matter how strongly we think "women in leadership" is a great idea on paper, in practice most of our daily lives and behaviors are riddled with bias against it.

So we continue to believe that leaders are chosen because they are most qualified, not identifying messages we receive all around us that disqualify women.

A former executive director of a major NGO comments, "There is this prime assumption that the men who are leading these organizations are really good. They're not. . . . Some are pretty mediocre. At the moment women are having to be very, very good to get to the top." When leadership qualities like depth of voice, commanding presence, and color of skin are what inch a candidate from "good" to "most qualified," despite their superior qualifications, it's nearly impossible for someone with a softer speaking voice, a smaller stature, or a different skin color to be seen in such a role. Women who reach top posts have almost impossible obstacles to overcome, including the rest of us overcoming our collective bias that men are naturally more qualified and suitable leaders.

It's true too that men self-identify as qualified for a new role when they meet only 60 percent of the requirements, while women require full qualification to even apply. But it is also true that women are held to a higher, perhaps impossible, standard when they do serve in roles of leadership.

What came first, we wonder, the devaluing of women and what they have to offer, or the devaluing of women by themselves?

In missional organizations, our history adds another layer of complication: men haven't just been the de facto leaders based on their biology. Scriptural interpretations and cultural practices have also justified blocking and disqualifying women from executive roles.

Just as communities and churches over decades have segregated women from leadership to caregiving, workplaces have done the same. How this is manifested in missional organizations came across over and over in our focus group interviews.

Charlene comments,

> I'm still shocked that motherhood and womanhood are seen as obstacles for women to be in leadership. Opportunities are held from women because at some point they may have a baby or may need extra consideration due to care for children. Organizations should just accept the fact that many women will require a season to have children. They should accept the cost of supporting women on maternity leave or during lactation time. These things should not stand in the way of her being promoted if she's qualified. By now, organizations should just accept it and make space for it.

The absence of constructs that support women in the workplace is, whether explicitly or subtly, justified by the belief that children are entitled to be raised by mothers who stay at home. In conservative Christian circles we still encounter the concept of a "kept woman." We've had conversations with men and couples who draw their sense of identity from the husband providing and the wife and family being provided for. We have also seen the burden of shame a man carries when, due to illness, unemployment, or some other reason, he cannot provide for his family. We've even encountered husbands who are ashamed of their wife's career because they believe it makes them look weak.

There are individuals who hold this worldview on the leadership teams and boards of missional organizations. How can a woman succeed in such an environment?

Constructs for women to succeed are often missing both in the workplace and at home, and this is especially true in our Christian context. As theological interpretations have preferred women to stay at home, so have economic systems. Between the world wars, new labor laws led to the establishment of the "family wage," where a man earned adequate wages to support his family, encouraging the wife not to work.

"There has always been a tension hidden within this ideology," states author Sarah Jaffe, "whether women were needed at home because their work in the home was indispensable, or whether women should stay at home because they were simply too pure, or too good for the world of wage labor." Professor Gayle Kauffman comments, "While there have always been women, particularly women of color, poor women and immigrant women in the labor force, the modern workplace developed during a time when our society emphasized separate spheres for women and men."

It is no wonder so many women are unable to succeed in the workplace; it was originally designed, through systems and constructs such as the family wage and ideologies like the male breadwinner, to keep them at home. And in missional organizations, theology and historical economic constructs are so tightly wound that they can't be told apart. Was it scriptural interpretation or economic benefit that first said, "A woman's place is in the home?" Or was this notion created in a dialogue between the two?

All the while women's employment is still considered an exception to male employment and female leadership to male leadership. This despite the fact women represent 40 percent of most countries' workforce, 50 percent in the United States. Organizational policies and practices like to pretend that women are at home. But women are not at home, they are working right inside our missional organizations.

A Note on Leadership and Women of Color

It's important to call out here the disparity between women of color and White women. This is a painful legacy that manifests in a continued pay gap and lack of representation, among other outcomes. While we have included vignettes and interviews with women of all backgrounds, we, as White women, do not presume to speak for women of color. And the sector *must* hear from women of color. We personally continue to learn more about systemic racism in our organizations and the ways it has held women and men back in unjust and criminal ways. We believe that if organizations adapt the approach and principles of a culture of belonging we have laid out in this book, they can create more welcoming environments for both women and other minority leaders. However, this will not, and should not, happen without dialogue with—and leadership of—women of color.

WOMEN'S ISSUES

Women of color face unique obstacles. "Why are there not more brown and black women at the CEO level?" writes a CEO of a secular INGO. The organization she leads focuses on improving sexual and reproductive health in the Global South, a key women's rights issue. In one high-level meeting with peer organizations, she says, she "faced a wall of white men." She concludes, "Certainly, men are and should be part of that movement, but they are over-represented in leadership positions, including at the very top."

The irony of this should not be lost on anyone. Why are White men at the very top levels of organizational leadership speaking on behalf of women and on issues that affect women?

One of the five female CEOs among the top fifty Christian nonprofits comments, "Quite simply, the pool of entry level candidates for a Christian nonprofit are majority white and privileged. There is significant work needed to help expose economically poorer and non-white communities to this type of work—which they would naturally be empathetic to and well-suited for—and to provide the mentoring and support needed to help enlarge the pool of diverse candidates within the U.S."

Missional organizations must work not just to find out what is preventing the progress of women and minoritized people inside our walls; they must also find out what obstacles nonwhite candidates encounter outside our walls that prevent them from joining our organizations—and then break down those obstacles. The answer to the diversity issue for organizations cannot continue to be, "We couldn't find any qualified applicants." Instead, organizations have an invitation to come up with brand-new strategies to recruit people of all backgrounds, and that includes taking a critical look at the criteria of what a successful applicant looks like.

The missional sector desperately needs qualified women to lead in the years to come. This is not only a justice issue. Our ability to secure future funding and programmatic relevancy depend on it. For the past decade, the best development practices tell us that solutions and programs must be locally led and birthed among the people who are most impacted by the problems. This means not only centering women and minoritized people in program funding, design, and implementation, but centering the very populations our programs serve in our neighborhoods and global programs. Refugees must be at the center when resettlement services are designed. Local faith leaders must sit around the table when organizations discuss what religious education programs to roll out in communities. And women must certainly be involved when decisions around policies and programs impacting women's health are being decided on.

The Challenges Women Face

- Women and girls have unique health needs, but they are less likely to have access to high-quality health services, essential medicines and vaccines, maternal and reproductive health care, and insurance coverage for routine and catastrophic health costs, especially in rural and marginalized communities. Restrictive social norms and gender stereotypes can also limit women's ability to access health services.

- The provision of sexual and reproductive health services—including healthy timing of pregnancies, maternal health care, and services related to gender-based violence—is central to the health, rights, and well-being of women and girls.

- The concerted effort of the global community continues to reduce preventable child deaths. Notwithstanding the progress, some 5.3 million children died before reaching five years of age in 2018 alone, and nearly half of those deaths, or 2.5 million, occurred in the first month of life.

- Before the Covid-19 pandemic, girls from the poorest households faced major obstacles to education: 44 percent of girls compared to 34 percent of boys from the neediest families have never gone to school or dropped out before completing primary school.

- Around the world, women earn less, save less, and hold less secure jobs; therefore their capacity to absorb economic shocks is less than that of men. In developing countries, 70 percent of women's employment is in the informal economy, with no protections such as sick leave or time off to care for children or aging parents.

- It is estimated that one in three women will experience violence during their lifetime.

- At least 200 million girls and women in thirty-one countries have experienced female genital mutilation (FGM) in violation of their human rights. In 2020 it was estimated that 34 percent of girls age fifteen to nineteen had undergone FGM.

- Women have a 27 percent higher risk of facing food insecurity than men. Their willingness to sacrifice their own food intake for the sake of feeding their children, as well as their high percentage as single head-of-household status, both contribute to this reality.

- Women are 14 percent more likely to die in natural disasters than men. Human trafficking and sexual and gender-based violence increase in their aftermath.

• • •

As we sat through one presentation after another during the 2021 NGO Committee on the Status of Women conference, Zimbabwean gender advocate and policy adviser Nancy Kachingwe made a poignant statement: "Are we really talking to the decision makers when we meet here? Are these the rooms where macroeconomic decisions are made? I think not. Therefore we need constant, relentless sensitization of those making decisions."

We agree with Kachingwe. The problem is that many of the discussions focused on the role of women are happening without current decision makers in the room.

The missional organization's "problem with women" is not just a women's problem to be solved by all-women panels and discussion groups. Current leaders, who statistically are mostly men, desperately need to participate in the conversation and mine for solutions with us.

The rigor with which missional organizations have created innovative development practices and cultivated transformational development principles must also be applied to creating organizations of belonging. Perhaps the last frontier of transformational development needs to be the transformation of the organization from the inside. It's time. It's long past time.

CHAPTER TWO

A CULTURE OF BELONGING

A s I (Eeva) write this, a pile of reference books sits next to me. Among them is *Feminist Fight Club: A Survival Manual for a Sexist Workplace.* Strong title no doubt, and not exactly one that invites the collaboration of male colleagues. Still, most women can tell their own stories of when work felt less like a meaningful career and more like a fight club.

There are the women who were hired as senior executives because of their creative ideas and leadership qualities only to be dismissed after a year or two for "obstinance" or "difficult personality." There are the junior women hired as team contributors whose main job functions ended up being notetaking and making coffee. There are the analytical women who were pushed to the side as "naysayers" or because of their uninspiring communication style. There are the older women who were deemed irrelevant and out of touch. There are the mothers trying to desperately figure out what to do with a sick child on a day when she cannot miss a presentation. Women of all kinds— including this one—will tell you how many of their days have felt like a fight.

Even if they say they embrace gender equality in the workplace, organizations are imprinted by historical and cultural norms from their formative years that continue to push women down. In missional organizations, women continue to fight for equal salary, a seat at the table, maternity leave, stretch assignments, voice, visibility, flexibility, platform, and influence. The list goes on. If women are not deliberately supported by men in these efforts, we must assume they are either being overlooked or outright opposed. Both have the same demoralizing effect, leading to withdrawal, passivity, ceasing to believe in God-given talents, and, at worst, giving up altogether.

How much human capital is being wasted because life inside missional organizations feels like a battle?

Not long after Sarah joined a leadership team, she noticed that her contributions were being undervalued and downright dismissed because of how she presented herself. "I had always contributed to teams with empathy and humor. My style was to keep relationships respectful and caring no matter how serious the issues we were dealing with." She realized immediately that her natural style was not welcome on her new team. The top boss created an atmosphere where communication was intense and borderline hostile.

After a few years on the team, Sarah had lost her unique ability. She explains, "I stopped relating to people in my natural way and instead became argumentative and a 'straight shooter.' In the end, the cost was higher than just my interactions on the team. I lost a piece of myself, and I couldn't do my work well because I had to always be on guard to make sure I was saying the right thing and behaving in the right way. I became nervous and insecure. I loved my work because I loved people. And on that team, that important part of me was not valued."

A SYSTEMS APPROACH TO CULTIVATING A CULTURE OF BELONGING

These days, organizations want diversity and inclusion more than ever before. This desire is born out of necessity when donors and staff begin to demand it, but also from genuine growth many leaders are experiencing personally. It is a hopeful season as many missional organizations find new conviction for more diverse leadership. As a result, organizations turn to focus groups, diversity panels and committees, executive training, consultants, town halls, and countless other initiatives.

More often than not, these well-meaning efforts fail. At minimum they fail to have the intended impact.

Diversity training is a multibillion-dollar industry. The experience, qualifications, and skills of the consultant or team hired usually have no relationship to the success of the diversity, equality, and inclusion (DEI) initiatives, but these individuals often carry the blame when things don't change. The struggle is that organizations are trying to solve complex, multi-generational, and deeply rooted problems in a three-hour training or single diversity panel series, with very little decision-making power or budget to make a change.

A new and better approach is desperately needed.

We have structured this book in the same way we believe organizations have to approach diversity to make a real and sustainable impact: by pushing on several levers simultaneously. Research on gender equality in leadership tells us that to be effective, organizations must engage in the complex work of tackling this issue on multiple fronts: harnessing the leadership will to make a change, addressing organizational and leadership culture, adjusting human resources policies and practices, being intentional about leadership development, and adopting a policy for addressing ideological or theological misinterpretations.

Each of these levers must be engaged to create a comprehensive approach that will ensure that women and men can lead and work together, leading to better organizational results.

Often organizations try to adjust just one or two practices (press one or two levers) to improve diversity. They may cast a wider net and bring in more female candidates only to have them turned down by biased hiring managers. They may hire more women candidates only to have them exit within a few years—a very expensive reality—because the behaviors, practices, and culture are unwelcoming to their style. Or they might implement mandatory training to combat bias, failing to realize that bias is built into their policies and practices, affecting promotions, salary and bonus structures, leadership cultivation, socialization, and much more.

Those who hold leadership power hold the levers. If current leaders, who are the predominant creators and cultivators of the culture, developers of policy and practices, and visual and vocal models of accepted leadership, are unwilling to speak up about the theological position of the organization or resist making gender equality a requirement, the system will defeat individual efforts every single time.

Gender mainstreaming is an approach that integrates the pursuit of equality and equity into all we do. In our research we relied on sources such as the Minimum Standards for Mainstreaming Gender Equality, which were developed by leading global experts on gender equality for the nonprofit sector. This group of leaders and researchers recommends eight standards that are "clear enough to set a minimum level of quality, but broad enough to allow each agency to define what is appropriate for their organizational and programmatic context." While we affirm this approach, the secular methodology alone does not fully serve the missional organization.

A Note About Programming

Many organizations believe addressing gender in programming creates a gender-equal organization. It is one of the levers but not the entire approach. Programming is the actual delivery of programs or services missional organizations provide. Gender-sensitive programming includes program design, implementation, and data aggregation and analysis. Gender-sensitive programming is an area of expertise led by trained technical advisers in organizations and while we have not included a chapter focused on it in this book, we have included a list of suggested resources for readers who are interested in further study.

For the past four years we have participated in the Wheaton Network Initiative on Gender, Development, and Christianity, which has brought together women and men representing senior leadership, programming, human resources, fundraising, academia, and advocacy to discuss current issues and obstacles facing gender equality across the faith-based nonprofit sector. Leaning on the lessons from the broader secular NGO context, the initiative has also developed a set of principles that mirror the areas we focus on in this book.

As a group, we discovered that what was missing in gender mainstreaming recommendations and resources such as the Minimum Gender Standards was perhaps the most important one of all for missional organizations: our theology. In our shared experiences and stories, it became evident that unless we address underlying theological perspectives and practices on an individual level, efforts around diversity will continue to stall.

Building on the principles of gender mainstreaming, adding the theological component, and making the principles more appropriate for missional organizations all help this approach cut across the secular–faith-based divide. The gender inequality of the past century is cemented into all corners of the missional sector, from its theology to its leadership culture, from its organizational culture to its policies and practices and the ways it develops and rewards people. It's for this reason that gender equality cannot be a side project that leaders and managers simply parachute in and out of. We need holistic transformation across organizations, starting with the most critical—our own.

A CULTURE OF BELONGING

The United States saw a considerable increase in demand for diversity-related initiatives and investments from the nonprofit sector, including missional organizations, during the Black Lives Matter demonstrations that took place after the murder of George Floyd in the summer of 2020. The Women's March of

2017 after Donald Trump's inauguration, preceded by the #MeToo movement, also made an impact. There is a knee-jerk reaction to injustice after that injustice goes public. Informed donors, staff, and other stakeholders raise their voices asking organizations to become more diverse. Leaders' hearts are stirred by events flashing on TV or maybe personal participation in the movement.

Sadly, too often it takes external events such as sexual assault or racially motivated crime to shake awake those who benefit from an unwelcoming culture and to embolden those who have learned to remain silent in order to survive and succeed.

Our sector's track record shows that those first well-intentioned but frail gestures don't stand a chance of producing sustained change. Diversity efforts are inevitably followed by discomfort and chaos, making life inside organizations and communities uncomfortable. New voices and opinions emerge and begin to push against our comfort zone. It's as if we—those of us who benefit from the current order of things—want change, but we resist it when it begins to feel uncomfortable and like *we* no longer fit in.

Working through this discomfort is the work of creating a culture of belonging.

Belonging starts with the realization that our missional organization cannot do the work we are called to without the voices and talents of a diverse group of people. Plain and simple, we have to walk into boardrooms or leadership team meetings, look at the faces surrounding us, and say, "This is not the right group of people to solve the most complex issues of our day." The group in that room will continue to offer homogenous, well-circulated, and either risk-averse or reckless solutions to increasingly complex problems. The invitation is to prefer a diverse group of new voices over the familiar group we are comfortable with.

We need to ask how women and minoritized people around the table—or those missing from the table—would solve the problem. What life experiences do they have that would contribute to an entirely different result? What questions would they ask? What conversation are we not having because they are not here?

Gathering the right faces around the table is just the first step. Mere inclusion does not equal having an impact. Diversity advocate Vernā Myers has stated, "Diversity is being asked to a party. Inclusion is being asked to dance." To this we add, belonging has a part in creating the choreography. And belonging should not just involve learning the existing dance steps. We should be open to changing the tempo, learning a new rhythm, and celebrating a new dance altogether.

The invitation to belong should allow our personhood, needs, work style, and talent to change the "the way we've always done things." It should influence how shared culture, work, and agendas are set. It means *who we are* has an impact on how the organization functions.

Defining a Culture of Belonging

We define a culture of belonging as a culture where employees feel welcomed, valued, and safe to be their genuine selves. This culture is established by leaders who prioritize the individuality, well-being, and success of each employee and, in turn, employees who share the responsibility for the well-being and success of the organization.

MAKING PEOPLE FEEL LIKE THEY BELONG

Sandra Van Opstal has studied, written, and taught broadly about inclusion in the context of church leadership and worship, as well as in organizational leadership. Van Opstal's work centers on BIPOC leadership, and the insights she shared with us can help us embark on a journey from hospitality to mutuality. Van Opstal says,

> When an organization starts with hospitality, we still assume that there is a person in charge. That person sets the table and creates the environment we all participate in. In hospitality, we might say, "Come on in; you are welcome here," but we don't have any intention of changing how we do things. When an organization moves to solidarity, we start to identify with another's community and their practices of lament and joy; we join in each other's grieving and rejoicing. Solidarity is not a new practice or idea; the Scriptures continuously call us to it (see 1 Corinthians 12:26; John 15:13). With solidarity, instead of running from it, we begin to tolerate some chaos around the table. If the person who sets the table cannot tolerate this chaos, he might not be best

positioned to lead through the journey to mutuality. Mature organizations move to mutuality when they realize that they cannot find an effective way forward without diverse people. They begin to seek out a system and a culture where each person can participate at an equal level.

Mutuality is not just an appreciation for what the other person brings to the organization, which can lead to exploitation or a disregard of that unique contribution, as we see with "token" hires. Rather, mutuality welcomes a distinctive contribution that changes the community. Women and minoritized groups don't just represent "insider information," say organizational culture researchers Robin Ely and David Thomas. "They bring different, important, and competitively relevant knowledge and perspectives about how to *do work*—design processes, reach goals, frame tasks, create effective teams, communicate ideas, and lead. When allowed to, members of these groups can help companies grow and improve by challenging basic assumptions about an organization's functions, strategies, operations, practices, and procedures."

To create a space of belonging, organizations and individual leaders must engage in radical self-examination to discover what is holding them back. Tools like employee engagement surveys and exit interviews can provide helpful information about how employees feel about the status of diversity.

Still, this is helpful only if leaders allow themselves to view the "naked" and often painful reality of how the organization and leaders at all levels are doing. Some leaders or organizations never arrive at this level of self-awareness and continue to hold the whole community back despite enormous efforts and investments toward diversity. To paraphrase Van Opstal, leaders who have held the organization back are usually not the best to lead through the journey to mutuality. If these leaders can move to true self-awareness and humbly realize that God still has work to do in them, communities can begin to speak in transparent and candid ways about the issues that need addressing.

This transparency also welcomes individual employees to express themselves candidly and acknowledges differences, whether demographic (gender, race, age) or matters of deep-level diversity (personality, values, abilities). Rather than asking people to downplay and hide differences, organizations begin to glean and benefit from the differences among their people. Individuals start to show up as they are, not acting out some type of role they've been forced to adopt to succeed in the dominating culture. This creates a culture of safety inside the organization.

Early in my career, I (Eeva) had an experience that showed me what an impact safety can have on performance. As an immigrant, I spoke English as a second language, and while I was a fluent speaker, I was new to technical writing. I was tasked with compiling and polishing a high-stakes report, and I wanted to prove myself. I locked myself in a room for several days to get it done.

The one to review the report was the top boss, a PhD and a prolific writer. The email came the next afternoon: my boss was livid. Something had set her off in the report, and she had proceeded to edit with a vengeance. She red-lined my contributions, all my colleagues' contributions, and even her own contributions. "This is ridiculous!" she commented in a section that included her own excerpts. She emailed my supervisor: "I don't want her writing these things again. She's not a native speaker."

I spent most of that week crying in the bathroom.

The dust settled, and during my next several years with the organization, I wrote and contributed to plenty of reports. The top boss probably forgot all about what happened: blowups were normal for her, perhaps as a result of her ascent to the top levels of academic leadership. But I never forgot her cruel words. "I'm not a very good writer" became something I routinely thought about myself.

Fast-forward to another job several years later. I was working in a new technical area, and in my second week on the job, I was asked to contribute to a major grant with the rest of the team. My boss called me into her office. Pointing to her computer screen, she said, "Here and here, the writing seems a little thin. You need to work on the language."

"In my defense," I replied, despite my lingering insecurity, "it's my second week here. Can I give it another go so I can make sure I'm coming across clearly?"

She agreed. A few days later my boss commented, "Nice turnaround. You have potential as a writer on the team."

Just like that, I went from a not-very-good writer to someone with potential. With those words and a bit of direction and support, my boss unlocked what I was capable of.

What I experienced that day with my second boss was learner safety. Learner safety is a building block of organizational safety, a permission to engage in all aspects of the organizational learning process, including one's own personal contribution. Traditional thinking tells us we should feel shame and hide our inadequacies if we don't know how to bring A-level work from day one. Learner safety gives us the ability to grow and learn in our roles and allows us to fail so we can eventually flourish and innovate.

In his research, Timothy Clark has identified four stages of psychological safety in the workplace. *Inclusion safety* refers to the basic human need for connection and belonging and is developed through a sense of acceptance by others in the work community. *Learner safety* provides people the ability to ask questions, receive positive feedback, and have the opportunity to learn through experimentation and even failure. *Contributor safety* is our ability to contribute and make a difference through participation as our unapologetic selves. Finally, *challenger safety* allows people to challenge themselves, question the organization, and probe norms and ways of working.

It's a leader's job to create the conditions that foster all stages of psychological safety, including team members' ability to challenge. According to Clark, "Challenger safety is a level of psychological safety so high that people feel empowered to challenge the status quo, leaving their comfort zones to put a disruptive idea on the table, which by definition is a threat to the way things are done and therefore a risk to themselves personally."

Elise talked to us about challenging the status quo. She was a midcareer technical expert and team leader with a solid reputation. In her interactions with executive leaders she always enjoyed good rapport and mutual respect. During a presentation with the leadership and the board, she made a splash and caught the eye of senior leaders. Not long after, the leadership team shuffled structure and she was invited to join as a VP. The first year was a smooth one. Elise experienced a lot of inclusion as she joined senior-level meetings where decisions for the whole organization were being made—she was often the only woman in the room but felt comfortable because she had a clear voice at the table.

The following year the organization hit a rough patch, and its financial future became less steady. The team needed to make decisions about reductions in force and new strategic direction. Elise and her bosses didn't see eye to eye on some of the decisions, and Elise expressed her differing opinion. This didn't go over well. In the following months the relationships deteriorated. Elise felt increasingly that she wasn't being listened to and that the only way she would be heard was to agree with her bosses. The disagreement led to a complete shutdown in communication, and in the next round of reductions, Elise's unit was restructured and she was let go. The story shared about Elise behind closed leadership doors was that she was difficult, inflexible, emotional, and not a team player.

Elise was safe as long as she agreed with and supported the majority opinion. But when a moment of disagreement arrived, she did not have the safety to offer dissenting views or challenge the status quo.

In addition to being able to challenge, the ability to fail is also a significant component of organizational safety. Based on her research, Amy C. Edmondson concludes that safe organizations destigmatize failure. Rather than saying, "Effective performers don't fail," safe organizations reframe this with, "Effective performers produce, learn from and share the lessons from intelligent failures." A psychologically safe atmosphere gives people the ability to make a mistake. If an organizational community can accept a shared space of imperfection instead of fear and shame over failure, people have room to learn, grow, and innovate.

Freedom to fail is not just a psychological concept; it's also a biblical one. Jesus modeled these very principles with his disciples, who were sent out to try, sometimes succeed, sometimes fail, but always welcomed back and always provided a teaching moment.

Consider the impact of presenting your imperfect self but still feeling a sense of safety and welcome. Compare this with entering a space with open-hearted expectation only to be ignored or continuously undermined. We have all experienced what this feels like, whether in the workplace or other communities or relationships. It feels demoralizing and paralyzing. The difference is individuals who are energized and perform at their best, compared with those who are disconnected and disengaged.

Marissa, a nonprofit executive, shared with us, "Before I go into a meeting, I read the list of attendees and determine how I need to adapt how I show up in the room. . . . I know the ones who expect me to be quiet and only ask questions, and I know the ones who are completely fine when I bring my expertise and my A-game."

This is a game many women *and* men in organizational life and leadership are forced to play. They identify the most valued culture and emulate it, no matter how unsafe or unnatural it feels, no matter what it costs them personally or how it shortchanges the organization when it fails to receive their best ideas. When organizations begin to value safety for all, moving beyond making a select few feel comfortable or valued, people can start to show up in all spaces as their genuine selves.

LEADERS WHO MAKE US FEEL LIKE WE BELONG

Renee described to us the life events that had instilled belonging leader traits in her. The youngest of eight children, she naturally learned to listen and be perceptive while growing up. And an encounter she experienced at a young age made a significant impact. She tells us:

> When I was five years old, I fell off a banister and broke my arm. When my grandmother saw the malformed arm, she put on my Sunday best, and I knew something incredible was happening. The doctor she took me to see turned out to be one of the most compassionate people I'd ever met. He spoke to my aunt and me directly; he did not speak down to us. And so I decided at five years old that I wanted to be a doctor. I wanted to be like him. As an adult, I have reflected on this encounter many times, and it dawned on me that this physician who practiced in South Carolina in the 1960s during the turbulent civil rights era was white. I reflected on how courageous he was to treat African Americans but to also treat them equally and with dignity and respect.
>
> My son calls me an empath, and I can "feel" a room. I've learned to be a collaborative leader because I've had to play in the sandbox with so many people. My leadership style is trying to figure out what people

are feeling and seek to understand. I have also learned to be very measured. I believe this is the reason leadership teams need women, because we manage, adjust, and collaborate more. As an anesthesiologist, I'm also big on oxygenation. You don't want to be someone taking the oxygen out of the room as a leader. You want to oxygenate the room so people flourish.

No matter how determined organizations are to build a culture of belonging, the effort will fail without the participation of every leader and every individual.

When we think about who wields power in an organization, we often think of the executive team, not realizing that every person in the organization can influence the culture positively or negatively. Every leader with a direct report—even just one direct report—has power over that person's work experience every day. Leaders are the curators of the type of culture an organization will have, and they set the tone and model the types of behavior the organization will tolerate.

I (Beth) discovered this reality lived out in an organization I was consulting with. As they were trying to roll out a set of new cultural behaviors, the sentiment among embattled lower-level leaders was, "The day I see our senior leaders live these out, I'll follow suit." If leaders aren't committed to the culture and shared behaviors the organization is trying to promote, what's the point of pushing forward with the initiative?

Because of this need for leaders to model belonging behaviors, investment in individual leaders is where a culture of belonging begins. Leaders often serve in their roles because of a successful track record in some measurable area—a project executed, a fundraising goal reached, impeccable oratory in a high-stakes partner meeting. While these are valuable performance metrics, they don't automatically correlate with the ability to lead others well or draw out the best in people. Giving your best performance and leading others to provide their best performance are two different skills. And leadership skills do make a significant impact. According to a Gallup survey, managers and team leaders account for 70 percent of the variance between high and low employee engagement. When it comes to employee satisfaction, it's almost always about the manager.

Belonging leaders prioritize the individuality, well-being, and success of each employee. For leaders like Renee, who through her life experiences has learned to listen to and understand other people, this comes naturally. We don't all grow up in circumstances that prepare us to become these leaders, but we can all learn.

Too often we've seen organizations and executives put up with harmful and even toxic leadership behaviors and leave these leaders unchallenged if they and their units perform well and meet goals. Some leaders seem to get a pass for bad behavior, even though every leader should be required to grow and learn. In chapter seven we will talk about the importance of training all our staff, not just women, in the types of behaviors the organization is trying to mainstream.

Michaela, a senior leader, describes her journey of learning to us: "I'm wired to make quick decisions on my own and this is how I used to operate, but I have learned to make them with others because I know the quality of decisions will be better if we work on it together. I don't rush to make a decision; I've taught myself to resist the temptation just to move on. I sit in silence and wait for people to weigh in."

Charlie leads a team in finance. He shares,

> I get uncomfortable with what I used to consider small talk and conversations outside of work topics. I learned about the value of team members sharing their work and their personal lives and its impact on the quality of their work. I now make a point of reserving plenty of time in our team meetings for people to talk about their lives. This kind of "breaking of bread" creates community on the team. The more we know about each other, the more we truly care and can support one another. I learned to sit in the discomfort of small talk and now think of it as the most important part of our team meetings. It results in the trust we need when we tackle big work problems together.

"We'll struggle to be in each other's presence—especially when we're glaringly different—if we have no interest in maintaining or building a relationship based on love, trust, and understanding," writes Ashlee Eiland. Good leadership means caring for people—not just the people we feel comfortable with, but *all* the people on our team. If we serve in a missional organization and trust in a God who is actively at work, do we really believe that anyone on the team is there by accident or mistake? They have been placed there as people we are called to steward. We should steward them well.

The appropriate leadership posture within a culture of belonging doesn't come about as the result of a top-down or organization-wide mandate. While the organization decides what kind of leaders it will promote, it is individual leaders who create the daily experience of the people they lead. The belonging leader knows leadership is not about them; it's about getting the best out of those they've been entrusted to lead. This bottom-up emphasis empowers individual leaders to experiment with what works best with their specific team at that moment in time.

This approach takes more effort from a leader because the team's composition at any given point in time defines what types of communication and practices are needed.

Belonging leaders can engage in simple practices such as drawing more silent team members into the conversation and affirming their input, which increases their confidence in their own voice. They can learn how to care about people as whole persons and not just as means to organizational ends. They can regularly raise questions about whose voices are missing on each project, what perspectives outside the inner circle are needed, and how they can go about elevating those voices and perspectives.

Belonging leaders give people the opportunity to try their ideas, fail, learn, and try again, all while having their back with those in the organization who stand ready to blame or criticize. Isn't this the very essence of the "agility" many organizations strive for?

You'll often hear this style of leadership described as "touchy-feely," as if it were weak. But the belonging leader draws her identity from the one she has been ultimately called to serve, and this gives her the courage and commitment to exhibit the skills she sees modeled in Jesus' ministry. It's easy to practice the status quo leadership we see in many organizations—leadership that excludes unique voices, threatens dissenting views, and favors those who look, act, and sound like they do. This is not leadership. It is ego. And God has called us to lead in ways that leave ego at the door.

HOW DOES IT FEEL TO BELONG?

Cultures of belonging are not synonymous with the all-immersive corporate cultures that ask us to live and breathe our careers. Silicon Valley–style napping pods, executive-level golf clubs, overnight company retreats, corporate work-till-you-drop schedules—even our own missional sector's multi-week global travel that takes us away from our families—these can all be antithetical to belonging. While team-building and shared traditions have value, they can become hollow symbols and rites that keep us coming back for more, breaking our backs trying to "belong," while only a select few ever will.

There should be no right way to belong. Too many leaders reach for the phrase *culture fit* to describe someone who belongs in the way the dominant culture expects. But there are many who don't. What about those with complicated families or postpartum depression, those who care for aging parents or struggle with mental and physical health, those with different cultural customs, those who are verbal processors, introverted, or older? All should be able to find their place.

It is especially imperative to define belonging in this broad sense for women in different life stages and for minoritized people. Without this, 50 to 70 percent of employees are showing up to work daily having to "take it." *Code-switching* is the term used by women and minoritized employees who must constantly read the room to figure out how to adapt their language and demeanor to fit in. When people feel the need to change how they show up in a room, there is an underlying understanding about what the acceptable way to show up is. If a team member doesn't naturally "fit," we can assume they are working hard to do so. And this impacts how accepted and engaged they feel in their daily interactions.

According to a recent Gallup study, only 32 percent of US employees self-identified as being engaged at work. Thirty-two percent! And that number drops to 20 percent globally. While nonprofits fare a bit better than the for-profit industry, engagement figures track low across the board. Although organizational mission is a critical factor for employee engagement, it is not the most crucial factor. An average of 60 percent of women and men considered the top driver of employee engagement to be the ability to do what they do best. Better work-life balance and personal well-being are very important to

66 percent of women and 48 percent of men. The importance of work-life balance is even higher now: the top drivers of women's exit from the workplace during the Covid-19 pandemic were caregiving burdens and lack of flexibility.

People are looking to work for organizations that value their unique contributions, are flexible, and prioritize their well-being. Instead of spending time and resources creating a streamlined and highly controlled organizational cultural experience, we should be focusing on creating a flexible culture and serving each employee in their life stage and background. It's time to find new cultural values in our organizations, values that actually celebrate the messy, complex, diverse, beautiful, plentiful personalities and talents God has assembled in our organizations for his purpose.

Creating cultures that prioritize belonging is not code for tolerating underperformance. We believe the opposite of this is true. Later in this book we'll explore research on the correlation between diversity and higher performance. We'll also explore how the transparency required in a culture of belonging also creates transparency around recruitment, hiring, and performance management, which provides more clarity around what appropriate role expectations and good performance look like in an organization.

Lisette experienced this firsthand when caring for her aging mother while working a high-stakes project on a belonging team. Her supervisor had always expressed her commitment to people's life stages, so she didn't hesitate to ask for flexibility when she needed it. Because Lisette had, over several months working on the team, demonstrated her ability to self-direct and deliver agreed-on results, her manager had no issues negotiating a flexible, deliverables-based work schedule. Lisette would provide the expected work products, and her manager and other team members would cover her in team and stakeholder meetings if she needed to miss them. The agreement was centered around flexibility inside the boundaries of the shared work that needed to get done. Still, even with flexibility, the work pressure and her care work periodically became too much to handle.

"We agreed on an open-door policy," explains Lisette. "I could always go to my boss and talk about what was on my plate and how I felt. Often just that ability to process the work with someone brought me clarity and helped me see the next steps forward."

According to research by The Wellbeing Project, "A wholehearted commitment from leaders to bring well-being into an organization's culture and their active, attentive presence throughout the process are perhaps the two greatest determinants of overall success." An organization's emphasis on well-being should not be limited to HR initiatives around health and stress management, while those are fine tools that have their place. Rather, leaders can take an individualized approach with their team members so they can meet challenges, obstacles, and opportunities brought on by personal motivators and goals, diversity and cultural background, and life situation. This type of commitment from organizations creates well-being at another level.

● ● ●

Employee expectations are shifting. The millennial generation wants a work environment that authentically embraces diversity and inclusion in the same way they do within their social circles and networks. Missional organizations cannot dismiss this emerging trend; millennials will make up most of the workforce by 2025. This generation has seen glimpses of more equal gender roles in home and family life and aspires to live out a shared leadership model. Increasingly they demand equality in their responsibilities and work around home, parenting, and caring for aging parents. Millennials seek a balance of work, play, family, and community in life rather than intense ambition to climb the organizational ladder, as their parents' and grandparents' generations experienced.

The positive impact of these lifestyle choices is supported by ample research as young professionals enter the workforce with a vision for their whole lives, not just their careers. Organizations that foresee this change by investing in cultures of belonging not only pave the way for millennials; they invest in better workplaces for all. And it all starts with our theology.

Belonging organizations

- participate in a culture where employees feel welcomed, valued, and safe to be their genuine selves,
- have leaders who prioritize the individuality, well-being, and success of each employee,
- and have employees who, in turn, share the responsibility for the well-being and success of the organization.

CHAPTER THREE

IMAGO DEI—ADDRESSING THEOLOGY

During my time here, I have met many women who gladly serve in roles that are not leadership roles specifically because they want to have more time to focus on raising their kids and their family. Men, more often than not, are the primary breadwinner in their homes. It makes sense that men would more often seek out leadership positions with more authority and more opportunity for advancement so that they can be better providers. I really hope we are not trying to move the organization in a direction of equality of outcomes. That is not biblical."

This is a statement offered by a male colleague in a survey conducted by a major missional organization on gender equality. This brother captured in a nutshell the major obstacle women face: justifying an outdated worldview with theology.

The problem is that men—and many women—do not switch from

decades in church pews listening to messages about the "weaker vessel" or in homes where men were served by mothers, sisters, wives, and daughters to suddenly seeing women as fully capable of carrying the heavy burden of leadership. It is not just our Christian culture that is guilty of this; everywhere around us women are still portrayed as less capable of leading through difficult, strategic decisions, more emotional in the face of key relationships, and "aggressive" when they display stereotypically male leadership behavior.

Diversity, equality, and inclusivity in our organizations will go only as far as our worldview or theology allow us. Despite all our significant efforts to create a culture where each staff member can belong, a theology that is not founded on diversity and unity will keep pulling us down the road of sameness and exclusivity. As people of faith we continue to get this wrong, because our theology is intertwined with national cultures, our socialization, and our personal preferences.

If we want to create true cultures of belonging, we must first examine how our theology may be standing in opposition to our efforts.

JESUS CAME TO CHANGE HOW WE SEE OTHERS

Three hundred years before Jesus' birth, "ancient intellectual greats like Plato, Hippocrates, and Aristotle laid the foundations on which centuries of sexism were built. Although these Greek authors did not invent sexism, their writings contained ideas and arguments that were used to rationalize a particularly virulent form of misogyny," states professor Christia Mercer. "Once these ancient trend-setters devised arguments for female subjugation in the name of a *divine good*, it became self-confirming in the sense that women were taken to be naturally inferior to men, treated differently from birth, and trained to subjugate themselves, which itself further supported views about female imperfection and the disempowerment that entailed." The views our cultures hold on women are rooted in the worldview of ancient intellectuals, not in Scripture.

Jesus came to change that. Scripture states, "All of you who were baptized into Christ have clothed yourselves with Christ. There is neither Jew nor Greek; there is neither slave nor free; nor is there male and female, for you are all one in Christ Jesus" (Galatians 3:27-28). Theologian Lisa Sharon Harper states, "Before we were baptized, we saw the power differential and obeyed. Male and female. Slave and free. After we go under the water, we see only the image of God in all. We see only their equal call and capacity to exercise dominion in the world." In baptism we often focus on no longer being "other" from God, but too often we also continue to be attached to the power structures of this world.

Harper challenges this: "Baptism . . . connected the outward demonstration of washing clean to the inner cleansing of all implicit and explicit biases that were entrenched within the systems and structure of both Roman and Jewish society." All of our theology about women and men needs to be continuously and tirelessly washed clean of how strongly it is tied to cultural preferences and our own worldview.

A SHARED LEADERSHIP MODEL

God didn't intend for men and women to be at war when he created them both in his image, as co-laborers. It was in this intersection of women and men leading together that God declared the foundational words "very good."

When God saw that there was no suitable companion for man among the animals, he created woman (Genesis 2:18, 20-21). The word used for "woman" in Genesis is the Hebrew word *ezer*. Most of our Bibles translate this as "helper," which immediately draws our minds to roles that complement and support men but do not place women in a leading role. But *ezer* was no ordinary helper. The word is used twenty-one times in the Old Testament, sixteen of those referring to God as our helper. He is our mighty helper in our helplessness and certainly not our subordinate. God called woman by his own name to describe the kind of powerful help she could provide man and the whole creation.

Why should this strong and powerful helper fight to be heard and seen in our organizations? Why do so many organizations fail, despite their best efforts, to include and hear women around leadership tables? And what can organizations do better to start getting it right?

Scripture lays out examples of women leading and highlights the collaborative nature of Jesus in his treatment of women, whom he esteemed as co-laborers and co-leaders. As Mimi Haddad writes,

> While businesses and organizations are now realizing the importance of including women in the highest levels of organizational

decision making, the first human community—Adam and Eve—shared dominion together before the fall. And, the earliest Christian churches were ahead of their time when it came to diversity in leadership, including slave and free, Gentile and Jew, and female and male from around the ancient world. As we try to imitate their faith and vitality, we should confidently imitate their model of leadership, in which gender, class, and ethnicity were irrelevant.

The biblical mandate for gender was never for one to thrive at the expense of the other. On the contrary, it was that both should flourish, with work and leadership shared mutually. When discussion turns to the advancement of women, many immediately think the result will be the abasement of men. This is a dated and limited perspective. In a patriarchal worldview, power is determined by how a man measures up in his standing against others, whether other men, including other races, or women. God's design of equality doesn't place women, or anyone, in a position of being degraded but elevates all to a place of flourishing.

As organizations and communities, we should recognize that to reflect God's nature to the world, we must reflect being in community with one another—serving and leading together. "The narrative of creation in Genesis 1 highlights the community aspect of the image of God. God declared 'let us make man in our image,' then the creator fashioned humankind in his own image by creating them, male and female. This aspect of the biblical narrative suggests that humans in relationship with each other reflect the divine image in a way that the solitary individual human being cannot," states theologian Stanley Grenz.

No scriptural case can be made that Jesus valued men or their contributions over women. Throughout his ministry Jesus taught that a woman's value resides in her response to God's revelation and not in her gender or role. He engaged women leaders in a new covenant, and he consistently challenged those who tried to devalue women. He spoke directly with women. He first disclosed his identity as Messiah to a Samaritan woman and allowed women to sit at his feet as disciples, preparing them for their roles as teachers and evangelists.

In his final moments, and in the greatest priestly anointing in history, Jesus was anointed for his work on the cross by a woman. When his disciples showed disapproval, Jesus rebuked them and said of Mary, "By pouring this perfume over my body she's prepared me to be buried. I tell you the truth that wherever in the whole world this good news is announced, what she's done will also be told in memory of her" (Matthew 26:12-13). In his first appearance after his death and burial, Jesus appeared to women and sent Mary to share the good news with other disciples (see John 20:17-18). In so doing she becomes the "apostle to the apostles."

Jesus modeled leadership that recognized the significant and important role of women in ministry. The work could not be accomplished by men alone. Nor did Jesus reach out to men of his own culture and race alone but to all who would come. A monogendered, monocultured leadership table does not reflect God's divine image to the world. Women and men created in his image, called for his purposes, leading together—this is the true reflection of the divine calling.

ORGANIZATIONAL STANCE

Still, organizations hold views either consciously or subconsciously about women that hinder their inclusion in leadership roles. This is partially due to the absence of a clear organizational stance, whether in policy or theological position, on the inclusion of women at all levels. Without this organizational stance, leaders can carry their own worldview or theological interpretation right through the front doors into their work communities.

"Even though our organization says women can be leaders, we have men who refuse to meet with women one-on-one and refuse to allow them to do any presentations where Scripture is involved because of their personal views on women." This all-too-common experience was described frequently in the focus groups and interviews we conducted for this book. This behavior is harmful to women because it excludes them from mentorship and socializing opportunities with men who determine the next promotion or salary increase.

In certain evangelical circles, opinions and statements against women's leadership are still very much a part of the public discourse. John MacArthur authoritatively said that Beth Moore, a theological scholar and speaker with a huge impact, should "go home" to an almost all-male audience, and they chuckled. John Piper made his case for why women shouldn't be seminary professors by stating, "If you strive to carve up teaching in such a way that it's suitable for women, it ceases to be suitable as seminary teaching." On more than one occasion during the election campaign of 2020, vice presidential candidate Kamala Harris was accused by evangelical leaders of having a "Jezebel spirit," whether alluding to her role as a woman in leadership, her racial background, or both.

These examples are just the tip of the iceberg of how women in leadership roles are diminished and brutalized. It is still impossible for many men from certain churches and denominations to see a woman as a leader.

This worldview can easily influence how leaders view women on their team—necessary to the work but not leadership material—and it is prevalent everywhere in missional and faith-based organizations. The cost of failing to check our theology around women's genuine participation is beyond quantification. We should assume that it is a significant—perhaps *the* most significant—cost to our organizations.

THE IMPORTANCE OF A THEOLOGICAL STATEMENT

"We need a policy or statement that distinguishes that this organization is not a church and there are no theological barriers to women in leadership," states one focus group participant. Organizations rightfully embrace staff from a myriad of faith backgrounds, some even those without a strong faith conviction. And certain denominations still hold strongly conservative views of women in leadership. "It is difficult for men from very conservative denominations to see a woman as a leader. And these type of men are everywhere in missional organizations," a woman in one of our focus group discussions comments.

There is no such thing as gentle male supremacy. All beliefs that degrade women stem from the same core idea that women are less valuable or competent, have less to contribute, and can thus be considered more disposable. On one side of the coin is treating women in a way that disregards their contributions and leadership, while on the other side is sexual and gender-based violence.

Esperance, an NGO worker in the Congo, discussed this continuum of thought: "We live in a society which has become very violent—and where women are considered as prey. This is likely a result of our culture, which considers women to be incompetent and restricts their rights to almost everything, including inheritance, access to school, and even their own bodies." Both extremes stem from the same theological roots that silence women and keep them from advocating for themselves.

Megan, an international aid worker, shares her story with us: "Part of my role representing programming in a geographic region was to speak to churches about that work. When I traveled in certain parts of the United States, I felt a lot of resistance; pastors and church leaders kept deferring to the men on my team, even though they didn't have any expertise in programming or the region. When I had gotten the role, I was celebrated as the 'first woman to head a region,' but when the organization was met with resistance to me in this role, they didn't back me up. My boss told me that the pastors were uncomfortable talking to me and asked for a man to come instead. My leaders said that they understood the pastors' perspective; they just didn't want to talk about money with a woman. It's like they were all about empowering me—but not at the expense of the bottom line."

This organization's leaders were okay with advocating for vulnerable people across the world, but they did not acknowledge the vulnerable position of their own staff member as a woman in a cultural context that respected only men as leaders.

Without a statement declaring the organization's official position, it is left to the discretion of individual leaders to decide how they interpret and prioritize belonging. This ends up sabotaging the whole organization and its best intentions for a belonging leadership model and the empowerment of women. These same missional organizations and individual leaders forget their first model of leadership, Jesus, who understood and promoted the significant role women played in his ministry.

Instituting a gender equality policy outlines for leaders an organizational stance on the hiring, inclusion, and promotion of women. No debate is needed. We have seen organizations take this a step further and establish a theological statement defining how women are to be treated and perceived in the organization, despite people's own theological interpretations on the issue.

If an organization holds a traditional theological position that bars women from leadership—and some truly do—this also has to be communicated explicitly. It is only fair for women who aspire to lead to know from the beginning if an organization has no intent of promoting them into leadership positions.

THEOLOGICAL STATEMENTS ON GENDER

When organizations realize they can no longer do the work they are called to with one hand tied behind their backs—without fully empowering women—a theological or policy statement is a good place to start. As a collective at the Wheaton Network Initiative, we recommend that organizations ask themselves the following questions as they begin their journey:

- Do we have a clear statement that expresses the value and contributions (and limitations, if they exist) for women and men?

- Are our theological commitments clearly communicated (and easily available) to external and internal audiences and reflected in our strategic plans, values, and priorities?

- Does our policy statement acknowledge the importance of organizational structures and discuss the need for balance between women and men in leadership roles across the organization?

Earnestly seeking answers to these questions will help clarify the answer to the question, Can women succeed here? We've outlined in this chapter why an organizational stance is so important, despite favorable or unfavorable views on gender equality held by individuals. To create a brand new culture of belonging, a public and shared statement advances organizations beyond opinions at the level of each executive and organization. We move from continuous debate to uprooting hurtful and harmful practices.

Many missional organizations take this step further, from grappling with and creating a theological statement to training staff in shared leadership. Many excellent resources are available, and we have included a list of resources in the suggested reading appendix at the end of the book.

Before we can pull on the other levers of belonging, we must first examine what we truly believe about the role women should play in our organization.

We've discussed how this idea may be countercultural to many people of faith. But efforts to enhance belonging will continue to fail unless organizations are willing to take a public stance on the inclusion of women.

Belonging organizations that address theology

- bravely examine cultural and theological misinterpretations that hold women back from leadership,
- acknowledge and challenge current leaders who may hold beliefs that intentionally hold women back from leadership and influence,
- and adapt and train staff in an organizational theological or policy statement that expresses the opportunities women will have inside the organization, despite the differing beliefs staff members may hold.

Creating a Statement for Gender Equality

Many missional organizations include gender statements on their websites. These organizations have done the deep work of investigating Scripture on this matter, and they have determined to value those they serve as well as those within the organization who serve others. By clearly stating a position on gender, these organizations have made it possible to reference this position in their leadership development efforts, promotional practices, and supervisory and management behaviors. Additionally, during the hiring process, such a statement clearly communicates whether a woman will be welcome as a leader in their organization. In many ways, by sharing these gender statements in a public manner, it allows others to hold these organizations accountable.

The Wheaton Network Initiative on Gender, Development and Christianity uses the following language for their statement:

> We affirm the Biblical truth that from the beginning, man and woman were created in God's image to govern the world side by side (Genesis 1:26-28). The flourishing that God intended through woman and man's mutual service and leadership was undermined by their sin. As a result, their shared rule deteriorated into male dominance (Genesis 3:16) which is not God's ideal. The equal value of women and men's shared governance is demonstrated throughout scripture and

particularly in the practices of Christ and His teachings. We commit to being explicit and transparent about our commitment to the equal value of women and men.

When assessing statements on gender and equality, we suggest looking for the following components:

- Women and men are created equal and each bear God's image—*imago Dei*.

- Every human being has dignity, worth, and equal value.

- The diversity of the organization is a representation of the theological conviction that every person is created in the image of God.

- God works through all genders, ages, and cultures, and therefore representation is needed in organizations.

- To represent the diverse voices of the people being served, a diverse staff is required.

- Women are created to lead as well as men are, and the organization is committed to providing equal opportunities for women and men.

CHAPTER FOUR

A CLEAR CASE

Weerelentlessly pursue God's best design for missional work, yet we have missed the best design of them all: women and men working side by side. The work of diversity and inclusion is not just a great idea, or the latest and trendiest idea. It's God's idea; it has *always* been God's idea," states diversity teacher and advocate Nikki Lerner.

It would be great if we could leave the argument here. We wish saying, "It's God's idea" would make a compelling enough case for organizations to

embrace and pursue shared leadership. But we know it's not enough. We know this from the dozens of organizational leaders we speak with who say to us, "We know this is important, but show me the data for why I should care." So before we explore the rest of the levers that create a culture of belonging, we will take a few pages to focus on the *clear case* for why a shared leadership model is so important.

The research we explore demonstrates that organizations will be held back from reaching their fullest potential if they continue to embrace homogenous and outdated leadership models. Instead, organizations must embrace shared leadership. It is a biblical mandate. It is good for our health and families. It is good for business. It is good for decision making and innovation. It is good for stakeholder engagement. Key areas that organizations are looking to grow in are impacted by a shared leadership model that acknowledges and embraces the positive impact of all types of voices and styles. And if the missional sector refuses to enter and stay in the ongoing, global conversation around diversity and inclusion, it will fall behind in performance and impact.

GOOD FOR OUR FAMILIES

Sixty-hour workweeks. Living out of a suitcase 30 to 40 percent of the time. Strained relationships and marriages. Suffering families. For decades these have been all-too-common markers of life as a missional executive. It is as if the flourishing and fullness of life we seek for communities and families around the world is not the flourishing and fullness of life our own organizations and families enjoy. The organizational culture we have inherited and perpetuated seems to work against the very mission we are trying to accomplish. Why?

A major contributor to unhealthy work cultures and leader attrition rates is insufficient focus on the elephant in the room—leader burnout. We live in a culture where a leader is not supposed to show weakness, certainly not in the form of burnout. It's okay to talk about being exhausted or busy as long as we don't miss a meeting or a deadline. There is an unwillingness on the part of leaders to implement plans to mitigate executive—and staff— burnout. It is still considered a taboo subject. According to a Gallup study, well over a quarter of employees feel burned out at work very often or always. Unmanageable workloads and unreasonable time pressures are top contributors to this number.

Organizations end up leading from old paradigms of measuring performance by late-night emails, cars in the parking lot well past close of business, or that green "available" circle on Microsoft Teams. The line between commitment and workaholism is blurred further. When offered a promotion in this kind of culture, Margaret, a senior leader at a missional nonprofit, stated, "If that's what being an executive leader in this organization looks like, I don't want it." Workaholism represents an outdated and one-minded solution to how work is structured and what is celebrated and rewarded in an organization, and both women and men can fall into it.

Women and men alike suffer when a 24-7 work culture and uninvestigated hyperproductivity continue to be the gold standard. In this culture, suggest Robin Ely and Irene Padavic, "men have one primary identity: that of an ideal worker, fully committed and fully available. To fit this image, they must adopt the psychological stance of 'my job is all-important.' Nonwork identities, no matter how personally meaningful, become contingent and secondary." If this description sounds familiar to leaders and staff of missional organizations, we are surely missing the mark.

Women and men making decisions about organizational cultures together should consider the needs of all employees *and* their families. A leadership team where both men and women participate helps support healthy families in significant ways.

When women are around the tables making decisions about organizational policies that influence the family as a unit, the needs and perspectives of women and children and the realities of home life are well-represented. Many men elevate these issues as well, but studies confirm that women in particular elevate the needs of their children, families, and communities when they participate in decision making. Shared leadership also takes the burden off men only. Men too have significant roles outside work as dads, husbands, sons, and friends, and sharing the leadership burden together with women enables them to lean more fully into their other responsibilities and interests.

Many missional organizations work in programming for children's health—both physical and mental—in communities across the world. What if that same emphasis was given to living out that mission inside the organization with the children of their employees? In our programming we center the physical health, mental resiliency, and protection of children, should we do the same for the families of those serving in the organization? Missional organizations that have cultures that encourage and make space for men to reclaim all parts of their identities, including as active, engaged partners and fathers, can accomplish this. They are also organizations that will thrive in the future and attract top talent.

The positive impact of mom and dad's presence in the home through the important formative years of childhood cannot be overstated, nor can the impact of all caregivers' ability to engage with their children adequately. Even as we are called to serve the kids of the world, we are called to serve the kids inside our own homes.

I (Eeva) have often worked on teams that have claimed to be "family-friendly" but have held on to organizational practices, work and travel schedules, and workload expectations that have been far from the culture they claim to center. Hands down the best, most family-friendly environments, where I have felt most productive and empowered, have given me autonomy around my schedule and ability to decide how to prioritize my work. These organizations backed up their talk of a family-friendly culture with actionable steps.

A culture that centers on families has leaders who do the same in their own lives. If a leader says, "We're family friendly" but works unhealthy schedules, takes minimal vacations, and sends emails throughout the weekend, he sends employees mixed messages about what *actual* acceptable performance looks like. On the other hand there is the boss who publicly refuses to spend more than two weekends away from family on an international trip. Or the one who flexes around family responsibilities like schooling or illness. Or the one who makes sacrifices so their spouse can pursue their own priorities. These kinds of leaders model family-friendly behaviors for the rest of the organization to follow.

GOOD FOR "BUSINESS"

Numerous studies have been conducted on how diversity increases the bottom line. An international study of over twenty thousand publicly traded companies around the world from various industries and sectors found that having at least 30 percent of women in leadership positions, or the C-suite, adds 6 percent to net profit margin.

Another study concluded that "companies in the top quartile of gender diversity on executive teams were 25 percent more likely to experience above-average profitability than peer companies in the bottom quartile." Also, "Companies with more than 30 percent women on their executive teams are significantly more likely to outperform those with between 10 and 30 percent, and these companies in turn are more likely to outperform those with fewer or no women executives." The higher the diverse representation, the higher the likelihood of outperformance.

According to a study of S&P 500 companies, the twenty most diverse companies not only had better operating results than those scoring lowest on diversity, but their shares also generally outperformed the least-diverse firms. Another study found that corporations that embrace gender diversity on their leadership teams are more competitive, with a 27 percent likelihood of outperforming their peer companies in long-term value creation. The study concludes, "Different perspectives on customer needs, product improvements and company well-being fuel a better business."

Taking a purely bottom-line approach, our organizations could be more productive if more women participated in leadership. In the missional context we tend to skirt around using data from the for-profit sector to make a case for profitability and link it with diversity. Still, our sector borrows freely from the for-profit sector otherwise—executives, consultants, marketing approaches, business models—to boost culture, performance, and innovation.

Assuming the correlation between diversity and performance could also benefit our organizations, what would it mean in the organizational contexts we work in? Could it mean more women and girls empowered, more houses built, more people living with addiction served, more grant funding secured? What are the areas where we could experience growth through greater diversity?

Inclusion of diverse voices alone does not equal a boost in business performance. For this, organizations require mechanisms to help the best ideas emerge from a diverse workforce. These mechanisms include adequate and not just nominal representation by women in decision making. For organizations to reap the benefits of women's participation in innovation and key decisions, organizations also need channels by which women's voices are heard and accounted for. And how we view and foster disagreement needs to mature so that it is not seen as an inconvenience, impediment to timely decisions, or, worse, a threat to those who currently hold power and position.

BETTER DECISIONS

Diversity doesn't automatically translate into larger profits or a competitive edge, but there is a correlation between success and a commitment by companies to diverse leadership.

Commitment is the key word here.

There are a few unhelpful perceptions that make it harder to achieve diversity on leadership teams. The first is fear of conflict or the desire to avoid conflict at all costs. As Christians we don't always know how to disagree with each other in a healthy way because of the foremost desire to "be nice," or at least be seen as nice. This may lead us to think disagreement is a bad thing— it's conflict, and all conflict must be bad. Often contrary opinions are seen as a threat rather than a path to better business decisions. But research shows that when we move beyond our comfort zones and start to see that "the debate and unfamiliarity that come with diversity is an important catalyst for creativity and deep thinking," we can instead begin to see conflict as an asset and therefore invite it and celebrate it.

When someone across the table from us is questioning our idea or offering a different perspective, we can forget that this is a good thing. People who are not used to being challenged by women—or anyone else, for that matter—can feel anger. Being committed to diversity means working through these initial reactions rooted in discomfort and learning to embrace them as necessary.

A second misperception we encounter is that with diverse viewpoints it takes more time to reach consensus, and we don't have the luxury of time. There is truth in this argument, but the question is, is the fastest idea always the best idea? Usually not. Maybe we'd see fewer false starts or abrupt direction shifts in organizations if we had more debate among leadership teams when we create strategy and make decisions. The challenges we face as a sector represent a complex world that is only getting more difficult to navigate. Having different perspectives and experiences—those of women and men from different backgrounds, including from the countries and communities we serve—ensures we're not reaching for the simple and quick solution but considering all perspectives.

We prefer making decisions with people like us. It's faster and more convenient. As a contrast, according to a study, "having more diversity in a group creates awkwardness. However, it's the need to diffuse this tension that leads to better group problem solving. While homogenous groups may *feel* more confident about their performance and how they interact, diverse groups are actually more successful."

Lauren, who works as a project director in public health, shares an experience with us:

> My working style is always looking for the problem to solve. I think, solve the problem; the meeting is over. I work most closely with a technical adviser whose style is totally different from mine and she's also culturally from a different background. She likes to process verbally; she likes to process *all* the information. It frustrates me sometimes because I like to move things along. But when my colleague went out on extended leave, I felt less confident in my decisions because I didn't have her as a sounding board. I missed her analyses and deep dives into issues. I felt her absence in our decision-making processes. These days I ask her to weigh in. I think somewhere halfway between us is the sweet spot where we can make solid decisions.

The process Lauren describes points to highlighting, not hiding from, differences. It acknowledges the assets each person brings to the table and invites individuals to speak from those strengths. This is not an easy feat, because it "goes against many people's intuitions," states *Harvard Business Review*. "There's a common bias that psychologists call the fluency heuristic: We prefer information that is processed more easily, or fluently, judging it to be truer or more beautiful." Commitment to diversity invites us into the discomfort of walking in uncharted territory, but if we stay the course, we will learn something new.

The global staff of missional organizations are best positioned to understand the needs of global beneficiaries. Or, as any corporate CEO would put it, they "understand and think like the customer." In missional organizations the "customer" is not only the client but the donor, investor, and staff member as well. Women and men think differently, bring in different backgrounds and perspectives, and have different insights into the stakeholders we serve.

While most diversity research is conducted in the business sector, we believe the lessons apply universally across all types of organizations. When there is diversity of thinking around leadership tables, organizations perform better. When there is diversity in leadership styles, organizations perform better. When the perspective of the broadest range of "customers" is brought into leadership strategy, organizations perform better.

A study in Europe of over four thousand companies showed that those with more women leaders were more likely to introduce radical new innovations into the market over a two-year period. Other studies have found similar results, leading us to strongly assert that, given the challenges facing the missional sector in the future, the time for innovation is long overdue. Organizations need women around their senior leadership tables if they wish to survive and thrive into the future.

BETTER FOR INNOVATION

A country team I (Beth) was working with was struggling with a new community intervention that required staff to visit with female caregivers by going door to door, assuming these women would be home during the day. After several months the approach didn't seem to be working, and an all-male group wrestled with the setback. They pitched the scenario to a handful of women.

"Is it appropriate for women to receive visitors at home when their husband isn't there?" one female staffer asked. It was a simple question and a perspective the group hadn't considered. This observation provided the solution and paved the way for a new program rollout—go where women congregate and feel comfortable talking to strangers.

This simple example provides a powerful lesson: homogenous groups rarely have all the right answers—or even the right questions. To provide the best interventions and support the communities we serve, we need diversity in experiences and perspectives. People who are different from each other in background—education and life experiences, as well as race, gender, and age—bring unique information and skills to the task at hand.

It's easy to understand why these varying points of view introduce a better decision-making process. Seeing a problem or organizational challenge through the lens of multiple perspectives helps us find solutions that are not accessible to teams consisting of people who think in similar ways. Homogenous groups obviously feel better because they can rest in the knowledge that they will easily (or at least eventually) come to a consensus. "But when members of a group notice that they are socially different from one another, they change their expectations," states business theorist Katherine W. Philips. "They anticipate differences of opinion and perspective. They assume they will need to work harder to come to a consensus. This logic helps to explain both the upside and the downside of social diversity: people work harder in diverse environments both cognitively and socially. They might not like it, but the hard work can lead to better outcomes."

When we hear dissent and disagreement from someone who is different from us, research shows it provokes more thought than when it comes from someone who looks like us. Organizations that are committed to creating a genuine platform for a variety of voices avoid the pitfalls of groupthink and a singular dominating voice squashing out-of-the-box thinking. Research shows that companies that harness diversity in their leadership and workforce are "measurably more innovative" than those that don't. In companies with diverse leadership, employees are more likely to take risks, challenge the status quo, and embrace inputs from diverse sources. They are 75 percent more likely to "see their ideas move through the pipeline and make it into the marketplace."

Diversity supports innovative thinking in two ways. First, it builds resilience. A resilient organization doesn't lean on just one actor (such as the CEO) but on a broad variety of people and solutions when responding to change or external or internal pressures. Second, diversity feeds adaptiveness. Variety allows the organization to test different ideas and responses and select what is most effective in each environment.

A nonprofit marketing team recently shared with us that they had come out of their most profitable year-end campaign in recent history. Despite the Covid-19 pandemic and the financial pressures it had placed on many of their donors, the organization was able to increase their fundraising goal by 25 percent. The marketing director then pointed to individuals and specific tasks in nearly every department in the organization, describing how each had contributed to reach the goal. She concluded by saying, "We achieved this in this unlikeliest of years because of how our organization pulled together as a community." The marketing team was able to produce content that resonated with a broad audience because of the broad team contributing.

What would it look like if missional agencies were innovative solvers of the world's biggest problems rather than, as some people consider them, mere Band-Aids on the broken leg of poverty? What would it look like if our organizations became the archetypes of the very communities we seek to foster in the communities we serve? The solutions may very well be in our grasp if our leadership tables are expanded to include a broader range of problem solvers.

GOOD FOR ENGAGEMENT

A wealthy donor couple attended a fundraising dinner for a nonprofit agency. The program included a panel conversation to display the organization's programming. Upon realizing the panel was made up entirely of men (in the nonprofit's defense, they were not all White), the wife got up from her seat at the head table and made a public exit.

"Is anything the matter?" asked the concerned event coordinator.

"The time for all-male panels and all-male leadership is over," she replied.

The relationship between a donor and an organization is a two-way street. Major donors, institutions, government agencies, and foundations present requirements regarding compliance and reporting. Increasingly these requirements involve questions such as, "What is the demographic composition of your board and leadership team?" or "What is the gender ratio of your organization's staff?" Similarly, donors expect to see compliance around sexual harassment and abuse prevention, data aggregation and analysis by gender, and analysis of impact of programming on recipients. Donors expect to see whether funds are being used in ways that affect those in greatest need: women and girls.

Individual donors have a voice. While they can't necessarily make demands of programming models, they can walk away. Just like the major donor in our story, they can demand change and go elsewhere with their feet and dollars. Research shows that women are more likely to give to women's and girls' causes and give larger amounts to these causes. Informed donors look at composition of boards and leadership teams, program impact on women and girls, innovation around gender programming, and protection of women and other vulnerable clients—including against sexual assault and gender-based violence—and the overall long-game commitment to women's causes.

For many organizations gender diversity is an asset to their public image, helping to bring them closer together with employees, donors, partners, and beneficiaries, increasing stakeholder satisfaction, and improving brand image. Over 50 percent of an average organization's donors or donation decision makers are women, yet their gifts are being stewarded by leadership teams that are less than 15 percent women. It is no wonder many women have started to make their giving decisions around this key issue—women are giving to women's causes and to organizations being led by women.

Coalitions are being formed by women desiring to pool their donations and fund causes they believe in. And it's not just private donors elevating the issue; foundations and national funders, investors and international agencies are asking for organizations to report their internal gender equality statistics and diversity plans. If the missional sector wishes to continue to engage donors at a deep level, then creating belonging cultures and diversifying its leadership is becoming a critical necessity and a significant opportunity.

WHAT IS DIVERSE ENOUGH?

Supreme Court Justice Ruth Bader Ginsburg famously said, "I'm sometimes asked, 'When will there be enough [women on the Supreme Court]?' And I say when there are nine. People are shocked. But there'd been nine men, and nobody's ever raised a question about that."

Asking, "How diverse is diverse enough?" still represents a tick-the-box mentality rather than embracing the types of cultural, innovation, and bottom-line changes we have described here. When organizations start to embrace the breakthrough diversity can represent, we can move beyond thinking about quotas and targets. The real change we are talking about takes us far past "the one/the few" to as many hires as it takes to create a culture of belonging and move our sector into the future.

If we're looking for a number, most research states that a minimum of 30 percent representation will start to have an impact on business as usual. But really, in the missional sector, why should the number be that low? Consider this:

- More than 50 percent of the recipients or beneficiaries of the work of missional organizations are women and girls.
- More than 50 percent of the staff that serve in missional organizations are women.
- More than 50 percent of the people making donor decisions, even if their name isn't on the credit card or check, are women.

How many women do you think it would take to create adequate representation of the issues women and girls care most about? How many female executives are needed to break the long-entrenched cultures that have brought you to this book? "Just enough" isn't enough.

The inclusive leadership model we're discussing is a new, shared life in our organizations that goes beyond representation and cultivates true belonging. Living together in this way should feel different. It will come at a cost for some who give up a little bit of their voice and space to make room for another to feel welcomed—a cost those of us who are looking to reflect the kingdom of God are willing to pay.

There is no clearly mapped path of how we will get there, and things might get less than perfect along the way. If it feels uncomfortable, we're probably doing it right.

A belonging organization that understands "the case" for diversity

- knows that greater diversity increases organizational effectiveness and performance, resulting in greater impact,
- welcomes diversity of opinion and voices around the table because they result in better discussions and more innovation,
- and invites more women around the table not just to tick the box but to create the significant cultural shift we need.

CHAPTER FIVE

A RECLAIMED ORGANIZATIONAL CULTURE

According to a global statistic, 81 percent of women have experienced some form of sexual harassment during their lifetime, ranging from being spoken to with unwanted sexual innuendo to being sexually exploited or assaulted. The widespread nature of the problem became undeniable in 2017 when, on the heels of revelations of numerous sexual assaults by Hollywood producer Harvey Weinstein, #MeToo became an overnight phenomenon, shared on social media millions of times by women all around the world. Women from the Christian faith community responded with their own #ChurchToo, which also went viral. Suddenly there was strength in numbers, and powerful men, whether in secular or "sacred" spaces, were exposed for their often decades-long wrongdoing. Bill Hybels, Ravi Zacharias, Mark Galli, Brian Houston, Larry Nassar, Bill O'Reilly, Charlie Rose, Matt Lauer, Jerry

Falwell Jr., Al Franken, Roy Moore, Bill Cosby, Kevin Spacey—leaders and public personalities who were exposed in their misconduct represent just the tip of the iceberg.

On the job, too, the problem is pervasive. Thirty-eight percent of women have experienced sexual harassment at work, and according to the 2020 study Sexual Harassment in the Christian Workplace, one in six employees of churches and parachurch organizations have experienced sexual harassment, and 42 percent of those have no intention of filing a report of their experience. We may never know about nearly half of the cases that exist inside our own organizations.

It's also noteworthy that since the first Christian workplace study in 2007, the statistics have not improved but actually gotten slightly worse. The reason for this deterioration could be the backlash women have experienced as a result of the #MeToo movement. Instead of the collective shakeup we wish these revelations would have accelerated, women are experiencing assault of a different kind.

According to a Lean In study, senior leaders are now "far more hesitant to spend time with junior women than junior men across basic work activities. These include one-on-one meetings, travel together for work, or work dinners."[5] Instead of rallying around women and championing their roles in the workplace, organizations are tiptoeing around the issue, and again, women end up missing out.

Sarah, a focus group participant, explains the impact: "It seems that my organization is retreating back to the 'Billy Graham rule' era, talking about whether it's right for me to work and travel with my male colleagues. But I'm the one who misses out on opportunities. If we're traveling or if there are meetings with presentations, it's not my male counterpart who misses out; it's me."

In other words, instead of saying, "We're sorry you have trouble controlling yourself around women, Bob. We will miss you on the trip," many organizations exclude the women from the trip instead. Some men's inability to conduct themselves as professionals and stop objectifying women results in women's careers being harmed.

Mary, an African leader working in the humanitarian sector, also addressed unfair consequences when she stated, "I have noticed that if a man commits an immoral act, his behavior is explained away, and he is prayed for. If a woman does it, she is fired and talked about negatively across the sector."

How can sidelining of women be the cure for mistreatment of women?

A BRO CODE

Much of our leadership response depends on the routine practices at our disposal. Organizational communities are still riddled with remnants of the age-old "Bro Code." While pop culture references to the Bro Code are considered comedy—think *Seinfeld* or "bros before hoes" on *The Office*—for many men the code they share with other men, especially in patriarchal communities, still stands strong. Who can forget the infamous "locker room talk" released during Trump's 2016 presidential campaign, a conversation meant only to be bantering between two bros?

The purpose of the code is to make certain that men "have each other's backs" and implies that men will hide each other's bad behaviors. No matter how ridiculous, this unspoken code continues in every workplace. It's the blind eye or cover for the colleague having an affair or "innocently" pestering women. It's the laughter, even embarrassment, at sexist remarks that go unchallenged. It's solidarity behind phrases like "Boys will be boys," "He's just joking," "She must have been a willing participant," "It's his private issue," or "There's nothing I can do about it." Silence in the face of misconduct is Bro Code. Plain and simple.

In addition to informal (albeit cemented) behaviors, organizations have many practices and even policies that enable continuation of bad and illegal behaviors. In the book *A Church Called Tov,* the authors explore techniques churches have used to silence and smear victims when faced with accusations of sexual harassment. These include discrediting the victim and the credibility of her story, silencing individuals through hefty severance packages that come with nondisclosure clauses, gaslighting (including destabilizing the victim and her own memory of what happened), shaming the victim for past behaviors, framing the perpetrator as the victim ("What's happening is hurtful gossip and causing division"; "These are unfounded accusations by a few disgruntled former staff"), destroying evidence, and issuing false apologies ("I'm sorry if you misunderstood my well-intended behavior").

We have observed all of these practices in organizations in the missional sector. They may not have been used to silence claims of sexual harassment or abuse, but they have been deployed to silence employees who are unhappy in other areas.

If an organization routinely uses nondisclosure agreements and severance packages to get rid of senior executives, or openly shares unfavorable stories about them, how quickly will they begin to do the same with victims of sexual harassment to cover the reputation of a valuable senior leader? Boards and executive teams who turn a blind eye to organizational practices that silence or tolerate unfair treatment of employees should consider the long-term impact of these practices and question their legitimacy in today's workplace.

Sexual harassment is the most serious form of toxic power in organizations. "Sexual harassment is not about sex; it's about power and what somebody does to you to take away your power," states journalist Gretchen Carlson, one of the many women sexually assaulted by Fox News chairman and CEO Roger Ailes. An organizational culture that preserves a power differential is engaging in perhaps the most dangerous practice of all. A culture of unchecked power and absolute authority is a breeding ground for incidences of sexual harassment and abuse—or an entire subculture, as in the Fox News case.

I (Eeva) watched from the sidelines as a church with an unchecked male leadership model let a dozen leaders off the hook for shameful behavior and abuse of power in many forms, including sexual abuse of young boys by a youth pastor. It wasn't the senior pastor who groomed and assaulted the boys, but allowing power without checks and balances resulted in a leadership culture where a male leader could eventually get away with anything he wanted.

In a well-documented incident in Haiti, senior leadership of a major NGO's country operations paid for sex with local minors in the aftermath of the 2010 earthquake. Among these leaders was the country director. This is an example of how, in our sector, unchecked power can trickle down to the last mile and affect volunteers and beneficiaries in the communities we serve. A study by the Humanitarian Practice Network found that sexual abuse is rampant in the international aid sector and "represents a catastrophic failure of protection." According to this study, the humanitarian sector is failing to protect the very people it is entrusted with helping.

For every one incident of sexual exploitation and abuse that is publicized, there are dozens of undocumented and unreported incidents. The same study found that the most critical gap was the lack of organizational and leadership support for prevention of sexual exploitation and abuse: "Head offices had not given clear directives to staff in the field on prevention of sexual exploitation and abuse, or supported their directives with adequate guidance and training, and managers were not being held accountable for policy implementation."

Many organizations have policies to protect beneficiaries and volunteers, but without a plan to monitor adherence to policies, people look for loopholes and keep getting away with exploitative behaviors. The very people our organizations are mandated to protect become collateral damage in the face of sloppy procedures.

It would be an interesting and helpful discussion for organizations to consider the continuum of sexual misconduct: How do sexist ideologies proceed to microaggressions, sexual harassment, sexual abuse, and eventually rape? If one end of the scale is considered "boys will be boys" and the other end is activity everyone agrees is wrong and illegal, where is the tipping point when behaviors cross the line?

Sexual harassment can manifest in actions and words ranging from sending text messages of a sexual nature to disrespect of personal space and inappropriate touch. The lines between acceptable and unacceptable become blurred, but the effect of the behavior carries more weight than the intent.

It is sexual harassment if it feels like sexual harassment.

In the Haiti situation we described above, sexual quid pro quo (meaning "this for that") happens when a person in authority, such as a supervisor, demands sexual favors or a relationship as a condition of receiving or maintaining a job or a benefit. Harassment can also manifest as a hostile work environment, where continuous verbal, physical, or visual forms of insult are present, or it can involve a single, severe incident such as a sexual assault. Women who are victims of sexual harassment describe behaviors that became increasingly problematic over time, resulting in sexual exploitation or assault.

The effects of sexual harassment are many, including absenteeism, victims changing their lives to avoid harassers, and leaving the organization altogether. A recent study on the effects of harassment on women shows that most victims suffer from anxiety and depression as well, just like victims of sexual violence: "The body can experience sexual harassment as trauma and these physical symptoms can run the gamut, manifesting as muscle aches, headaches, or even chronic physical health problems such as high blood pressure and problems with blood sugar. In the long term, it could lead to heart issues." The impacts of sexual harassment stay with the victim long past the incident.

To create an organization that stands for safety and belonging, two things must be in check: the culture of everyday sexism it permits and the amount of unrestrained power yielded by leaders, the executive team, or the board. When these are permitted to go on without restriction, organizations and leaders can end up walking above scrutiny and start to consider themselves infallible and their actions justifiable.

SMALL, EVERYDAY ACTIONS AND WORDS

A microaggression "is a seemingly small assault on a person's humanity based on their identity," whether gender, race, age, or another marginalized characteristic. Microaggressions are also characterized by perpetrators not being aware of the harmful effects of their words or behaviors. Microaggressions fall into two categories: biased actions that feel discriminatory and comments that signal at best insensitivity and at worst derogatory views. While some microaggressions are intentional, most are just off-the-cuff remarks.

I (Eeva) have personally experienced microaggressions when someone intentionally mispronounces my name or when people tease me for mispronouncing a word. (I like that my colleague, who is also a non-native speaker, has gotten in the habit of replying, "Pardon me, English is my fourth language!") I also experienced microaggression when, during my two pregnancies, male colleagues felt at liberty to touch my belly or share with me unsolicited stories of their own wives and even mothers. While acknowledging women during pregnancy in this way is polite in many cultures, these interactions made me feel objectified as a "pregnant woman" and shut out of conversations with colleagues based on my expertise and professional inputs.

In her book *I'm Still Here,* Austin Channing Brown shares an entire day's worth of microaggressions she has experienced as a Black woman, including getting her hair touched without permission and being repeatedly mistaken for another Black coworker. While a White woman might be able to predict where she'll encounter unpleasant behavior—and can even begin to avoid those situations and people—a woman living in the intersection of many marginalized identities may experience microaggressions as relentless, unpredictable, and ongoing throughout her day.

In another example, Dr. Jeanne Porter King writes, "In my early days as a rising corporate professional, I lost count of the times that some well-meaning coworker noted that I was a 'twofer' for my company. This micro-aggression revealed their notion of affirmative action and their assumption that I was hired just because I am Black and a woman, and my company could check off two affirmative action boxes by hiring me."

Sexism is another everyday experience many women face.

Picture this. The weekly meeting is about to begin. As the team settles in, Rachael leans over to Mike and asks, "Wouldn't you rather be home raising your kids?"

Susan, on the other side of Mike, hears it and quickly looks down at her notes in embarrassment. Mike is silent. He just doesn't know how to respond, so he smiles and says nothing. Clearly Rachael doesn't think he needs to be at this meeting. He wonders if others feel the same.

As you read this you're thinking, "How absurd," right? The expectation would "normally" be that the woman would stay home and raise the children. Or maybe you would never expect someone to say something like this in the workplace. And yet. . . .

This scenario is true, except for the fact that the comment was made by a senior-level male leader to a more junior-level female leader. Others heard it. No one said anything. And the woman sat stunned and mortified, wondering, "Do others think the same way?" This is an example of sexism, gender-based prejudice, and discrimination.

Maria shares her story of dealing with sexism in an organization with an older male leader. Whenever she would speak in meetings, this leader would either start speaking to the person next to him, get up and leave the room, or, if on Zoom, get suddenly disconnected from the meeting. At first she thought she was imagining things, but after several months she knew she wasn't. When she discussed this unusual behavior with colleagues, they said, "Oh yeah, he's uncomfortable when junior women speak up. He can't handle it. It's almost a physical reaction, so he makes up any excuse to leave. I don't think he even knows that he's doing it, but everyone else knows."

Like other female colleagues before her, Maria started to feel insecure presenting in front of this leader and eventually asked to transition teams because of it. This kind of everyday sexism is all too common in our organizations.

The link between sexism and some cultural norms can present further challenges. Organizations that serve internationally are known for expectation of compliance to headquarter policies. Field offices are asked to follow HR guidelines, maintain donor relations, and implement uniform programming. And yet the same organizations are less likely to intervene when local gender norms do not foster healthy environments for all staff.

In my (Beth's) work developing leaders in many parts of the world, I have heard numerous examples of men with seniority treating women with disrespect and expecting sexual favors and others telling these women to "just go along," because it was expected of young women in the local culture. In many instances normal national cultural beliefs and behaviors toward women can harm how women are treated and valued.

Organizations are occasionally reluctant to impose Western cultural values on local offices when it comes to treatment of women and other minoritized people. It could be culturally acceptable to call women names like "honey" or "sweetie" or even for a senior male to make sexual advances toward them. Yet if a national director was borrowing from company funds, the organization would not hesitate to impose Western financial management values in that situation. If a senior vice president was hiring all his family members for jobs, the organization would not hesitate to impose Western human resource values. Why don't organizations place the same value on protecting female employees and stop calling that "Western values"?

It's a human value that women should be treated as equals and respected in their workplace.

ADDRESSING SEXISM AND SEXUAL HARASSMENT

Addressing these behaviors in missional contexts can be tricky. In Scripture we are told to "go directly to the one who has offended us" (see Matthew 18:15). In instances of sexual harassment and unequal treatment due to sexism, however, this rule cannot apply. Victims cannot be asked to go to their offender alone (as is still *shockingly* a practice in many churches and parachurch organizations). If there is a power differential between the offender and the offended, accusation can result in further marginalization and even retribution.

Rather, organizations need clear complaint and whistleblower mechanisms, preferably involving entities outside the organizational chain of command. Some examples of best practices follow.

Clear policies and training. "Do no harm" policies, namely, prevention of sexual exploitation and abuse (PSEA) and nonharassment policies, have emerged in importance in the past decade. Nonharassment policies are no longer optional or even secondary given how many organizations, industries, and even churches have paid the highest price for not sufficiently protecting women and minors. No organization that claims to care for its employees, let alone clients, can afford for a staff and volunteers who don't know what their duties and rights are in tolerating sexual harassment.

Making it safe to report. It's imperative that organizations create a safe reporting process and communicate it widely. This can include the involvement of an external company that specializes in investigating such claims or an ombudsman who receives all claims and keeps them confidential until they are investigated. There should also be a mechanism for monitoring and protecting the complainant's engagement in the organization, promotions, and opportunities provided. The unspoken reality is that far too often claims are made, and perhaps an appropriate decision is made after investigation to fire the perpetrator, but rarely is the victim cared for and their career tended to after the incident.

Changing the culture. Studies show that increasing the representation of women in leadership results in a decrease in sexual harassment complaints in the organization. Character development is another strategy we'll discuss in a later chapter. One study notes,

> The single biggest predictor of sexual harassment on the job is how permissive an organization is of this conduct. Permissive organizations are those in which employees feel it is risky to report sexual harassment, think their complaints won't be taken seriously, and believe perpetrators will face few to no consequences. This may seem circular, and in a way, it is—harassment begets more harassment—but it also implies an important lesson: cracking down on harassers—severely and transparently, and at the most senior levels—discourages the behavior across an organization.

Until we tackle toxic leadership cultures, the problem with sexual harassment will persist.

• • •

The most powerful weapon against harmful workplace behaviors is awareness. When individual leaders understand the statistical probability of these behaviors showing up in workplaces, they're less likely to think, "This could never happen in our organization."

According to a recent McKinsey study, "Managers play a central role in shaping employees' day-to-day work experiences. When managers begin to regularly identify and challenge gender-biased language or behavior, employees are several times more likely to say their company values people's differences and quickly addresses disrespectful behavior toward women." This presents an opportunity for male allies to step up when they witness occurrences of sexism. Tim, who regularly sees women getting interrupted at meetings, has made a habit out of calling it out by saying something like, "Jane, I think you were interrupted. Can you finish the point you were making?" This action is simple and nonconfrontational but gets the job done.

LEADERSHIP WE PUT UP WITH

When the question "What is good leadership?" is asked in a room full of leaders, we're likely to hear a list of dozens of qualities, behaviors, and skills.

It's not a surprise that we're constantly disappointed in leaders—we don't have a clear and shared understanding of what truly makes a good one. In the absence of a definition, we continue to select leaders who look like us or who we're comfortable with, and end up with the same. Same gender, same culture, same race, same leadership attributes.

"Workplaces don't work for everybody the same way because they were never designed for difference," states researcher Michelle P. King. "They were designed to support an ideal type of worker to succeed, and this tends to be a white, middle-class, heterosexual, able-bodied male, who, most importantly, is willing to make work his number one priority and engage in dominant, aggressive, assertive, competitive, and even exclusionary behaviors to get ahead." So we continue to tolerate the same toxic behaviors, even though they have not served us well in the past.

A friend tells us about a boss she had when she was working in a mission agency: let's call him Fred. Fred had decades of experience in missionary work and the respect of his denomination to match. Fred also had a bad temper. Now in the twilight years of his career, he had still never learned to deal with situations that upset him. Anything could set him off: a crying baby in the back of a chapel when he spoke, the secretary who didn't get him his lunch on time ("low blood sugar"), or someone who disagreed with him about politics or sports—his two great passions. When something rubbed him the wrong way he raised his voice and, if he became extremely upset, he shouted, whether in his office, in conference rooms, or in the parking lot. His voice carried far and wide across the campus.

The entire agency's culture was tarnished by Fred's exploding temper. His peers chuckled and let him get away with it, saying, "That's Fred for you." The older women on campus catered to his every need and scurried when they heard an episode coming—you know, sort of like you would with a toddler. Scores of young staff exited, year after year, traumatized by Fred's unchecked behavior. The attrition rate at the agency was sky high. In his fifty-year career only a few people had dared to call Fred out on his behavior.

At Fred's retirement party he received high honors and accolades, maybe a few shared stories and laughs about his "fiery temper." His toxic behavior made for a lovable story told in his honor. Fred relished a successful "ministry" while others became collateral damage in the process.

Fred's story is outrageous. What organization or community in its right mind would allow such behavior? Turns out many do.

A recent study found that "56 percent of American workers claim that their boss is mildly or highly toxic." Additionally, 75 percent of Americans say their boss "is the most stressful part of their workday." It's usually not the workloads that make work stressful; it is the managers.

Is it possible that with staff made up of "churched" people, missional organizations are predisposed to tolerate worse leadership behavior than many secular peers? Our evidence of this is anecdotal at best but an interesting parallel can be drawn from the popularity of Donald Trump among White evangelicals. Myriad books, podcasts, and articles have been published speculating whether bad leadership experienced in organizations and churches paved the way for Donald Trump's election despite his outrageous behavior. A study "based on a survey of people confirmed by public records to have voted in 2020, showed that Trump was supported by 84 percent white evangelicals in 2020, an increase of 7 percentage points over the 77 percent of white evangelicals who voted for him in 2016."

Have evangelicals learned to normalize abuse from their leaders? It seems that leadership behavior that would be—and recently has been—deemed intolerable in churches and organizational settings was embraced with open arms by many in the faith sector.

Dysfunctional leadership manifests in many forms, from absenteeism to micromanagement, from rewarding incompetence and underperformance to lack of self-awareness. At some point on the leadership journey, a wise, discerning leader turns up the gears of self-awareness. But for some this never happens. Instead of becoming aware of their own leadership pits, they fall into them. Leaders may become trapped by self-aggrandizing and selfish interest or unaware of the impact they have on team members and the organization.

In its least harmful manifestation, an unaware leader can become a laughingstock without their knowledge. They forget how many times they told a story of a past success or become focused on how they are perceived externally, not on how their team or organization perceives them.

This lack of awareness can also lead to advancement of personal goals, whether personal platform, money, future opportunities, or connections. At its worst a leader who has lost (or never truly had) connection with the welfare of the community will begin to exploit others. This is toxic leadership.

Toxic leadership behaviors in organizations are manifested across a continuum. At one end are intentional microaggressions and microbehaviors—things like interrupting, sarcasm, and backbiting—to overtly aggressive behaviors such as shouting, insults, violation of personal space, unsolicited touching, threats, marginalizing, humiliation, sexual harassment, and shaming. Toxic leaders may also be known for "kissing up and kicking down," so senior staff may miss the behavior. Toxic leaders can, in fact, be charming. They are sometimes preserved by fans, whether bosses or constituents who cover their rears and continue to take the blame for them.

So why do we allow toxic behavior? According to one analysis, "Leaders, even bad leaders, satisfy our basic needs for safety and stability, for self-preservation. To resist leaders openly invites confusion, upset and is demanding in a way that just 'going along' is not." Until we value belonging for *all* employees over perceived organizational outcomes of existing leadership, most followers won't want to rock the boat, and most boards will ignore that portion of the annual employee survey.

NEW LEADERSHIP SKILLS

In chapter two we described the characteristics of a belonging leader. They are a far cry from the toxic leadership models we have described here. Missional organizations have an invitation to increase their competency when it comes to identifying leadership potential and selecting leaders. As a sector, we have to become better at identifying good leadership skills.

High technical capability, the ability to raise funds, and successful marketing campaigns do not equal a highly successful leader. Leadership is a whole other set of skills. Researcher Tomas Chamorro-Premuzic highlights people's tendency to be seduced by the hero model—confident, charismatic, and even narcissistic leader personalities who don't actually lead well once we've been seduced. Chamorro-Premuzic finds that real leadership comes from people who demonstrate humility and integrity along with their technical competence. He identifies these leadership qualities as feminine.

Research from the past decade has identified qualities historically considered feminine as those most closely aligned with good leadership. In a study conducted among sixty-four thousand people in thirteen countries, feminine qualities surfaced as globally accepted leadership traits valued by people across the world. These include trustworthiness; honesty; having foresight and planning; being positive, dynamic, encouraging, and motivating; communicating well; being inclusive; and being a collaborator.

Here we must emphasize that drawing strict lines between women and men as feminine and masculine feels arbitrary. Valuing the biological and psychological differences between all is critical in valuing everyone equally. While the differences are real, qualities of feminine and masculine don't fall strictly within the confines of a person's biological sex, no matter how hard culture has endeavored to make it so.

We know men who display traditionally "feminine" attributes of emotional availability, care, and attention to detail, just as we know women who are "masculine" in their competitiveness, emotional coolness, or aptitude for debate in the conference room. The reason for this is that gender roles are predetermined in cultural contexts, and rather than representing reality, they often represent dated and patriarchal ideals that don't allow space for our God-created individuality. The ways masculine and feminine qualities are distributed in each of us is unique to each person.

Despite this, men and women are trapped in cultural ideas of femininity and masculinity. Our culture still says to men, "You must always be strong" and to women, "You must always be nice." Welcoming more women into leadership as their genuine selves doesn't just begin to shift roles for women; it shifts and allows for men to reject the roles they've held on to as acceptable, even in the face of harm. Men have suffered when only one type of male leadership is celebrated as suitable and are trapped in systems that celebrate only one kind of masculinity.

Co-leadership liberates women and men to serve in the fullness of their createdness and calling. The desire and ambition to lead can be honored in each individual and in each unique manifestation.

For example, while women are ready to make difficult leadership decisions just as men are, many women don't view these decisions as zero-sum games and take a more collaborative approach. There doesn't always have to be a winner and a loser. It makes sense. As little girls, most of us are taught to be gentle and to get along. Of course, we end up manifesting these behaviors in adulthood—they are ingrained into many of us.

For the past decade leadership literature directed at women's development has guided us to shake those behaviors and gain more confidence, have a louder voice, and be more assertive. Tomboys and girls who display less traditionally feminine qualities in general receive admiration in school and inside our organizations. Male leadership has still been the norm that women have aspired to. We wrongly reason that if women adapt to male-like behaviors, they will succeed.

"Conventional wisdom on the gender gap has focused almost exclusively on changing women so they acquire the traits and behaviors that will elevate them to the top of a corporate hierarchy," says author Marissa Orr. "Diversity doesn't happen by forcing people to mold everyone into the same narrow template. It happens exactly the opposite way: by letting people be themselves. It happens by holding up truth and objectivity as the values that govern our organizations, so we can better see the full scope of diverse talent sitting right before our eyes."

How can organizations begin to have more women in leadership—women who are displaying their genuine voice at the table? No big surprise here: organizations need to consciously hire and promote more women.

Women are more likely to pursue leadership roles if they see other women accepted as leaders. We traditionally think of motherhood or other care responsibilities as the main limitation for women to pursue leadership, but it turns out it's more important for women to see other women living out the seemingly impossible—combining a career with life responsibilities.

Audrey, a nonprofit leader and a mother of two preschool-aged boys, shares her experience of leaving her firstborn at daycare: "He cried heartbreakingly, and I shook and cried in the car after dropping him off. My stay-at-home friends' comments, even those made by my own mother, made me doubt my decision. It wasn't until I spoke to women at my job, others who had lived through it, that I felt that I was making the right decision and no longer felt overwhelming guilt." Having role models made the difference.

Eighty-five percent of women in their thirties and forties who work for companies making progress with gender equality state that they desire a leadership position. On the other hand, if women receive signals from their organization that there is no pathway to leadership no matter what, they are more likely to leave or downgrade into a different role within the organization. The data shows that if women cannot see themselves reflected in leadership or don't see a future leading in the organization, they stop trying.

The greatest investment organizations can make is to promote female leaders and set them up for success. In practice this translates to three types of commitments from current leaders:

- For a new female executive to succeed, she must have absolute executive buy-in and sponsorship for as long as a new male executive would enjoy the same, if not longer. We can't count the number of times women leaders have been thrown under the bus in private executive conversations, especially when things don't go as planned. It appears that executive leaders don't have female senior leaders' backs, and as soon as things start to go in the wrong direction, whether with finances, relationships, or outcomes, female leaders are considered dispensable.

- For a new female executive, the parameters of what success looks like must be comparable to or even more expansive than that of her tenured peers. We have witnessed instances of assignments that are high-risk to achieve—also known as "glass cliff" assignments—and when they are not achieved, grace periods and opportunities to pivot are not extended. Current executives don't seem to have the same pressure and can miss the mark year over year, with grace reasonably extended (as it should be).

- Women must be given the space to lead from their own natural leadership style instead of being challenged if she is either "too nice" or "too assertive." If a female leader turns out to be "too assertive," for example, current leaders must challenge their expectation and comfort zone. Maybe it's okay for a female leader to assert herself in ways our organization is not used to, and maybe it's we who need to learn and grow—not the other way around.

● ● ●

Women are not perfect leaders. We are held back by our fears and leadership traps just as men are. For example, organizations may assume that hiring a woman or two will automatically lead to more organizational diversity, and while there is some evidence of that, many women who reach leadership tables do not automatically advocate for each other but end up carefully protecting their "slice of the pie." Others adapt to the masculine culture to ensure they stay at the table, thus not making a positive impact on the organization. Women also display what's known as "the queen bee" syndrome, which means they enjoy their leadership role and placement so much that they refuse to sponsor or promote other women because they see them as a threat. Again, this is a scarcity mentality: "If another woman gets some, I get less."

To overcome these leadership traps women need the support of other women *and* men.

Missional organizations need to become places where people can innovate, try, fail, get up, and try again.

This is particularly important for women. As women enter the leadership space in greater numbers, they need space to fail just as men have had that space. This doesn't mean just hiring women for "glass cliff" assignments, where they are promoted to leadership during periods of crisis or downturn, when the chance of failure is highest. It means giving women as many new and fair chances as men have been given.

HEALTHY RELATIONSHIPS

Women and men are called to lead together. At that unique intersection lies the leadership union God put in place in the book of Genesis. At that intersection also lies the full understanding of the work at hand, the asking of the complete question, the recognition of the answer and service and support one can give to the other. "Debates over superiority and inferiority die on the doorstep. The issue is not how we compare to one another but how we measure up to God's standard," comments author Carolyn Custis James.

This translates to a celebration of the healthy interaction between women and men: leaders who mentor women without stigma or fear (of appearances or themselves), biological and psychological differences acknowledged and welcomed at the table, women acknowledged as leaders because of the relationships we share. We begin to know and respect one another deeply.

Missional organizations are uniquely positioned to promote healthy relationships between women and men. Scripture offers us a model of this when throughout the New Testament the apostle Paul uses sibling language over one hundred times, more than any other term. Drawing on the social meaning of family relationships in the time of Scripture, he emphasizes the deep emotional bond he wants us as fellow Christians to have.

"God's people ought to have the same sibling solidarity and exclusive allegiance as a biological family," asserts New Testament scholar Joseph Hellerman. When understood in a cultural context in which a family offered physical and financial protection and safety, the case for siblinghood is a compelling one. Siblings looked after one another.

When as leaders we rely on bias and stereotypes about male and female— or Greek and Jew, for that matter—we miss out on the greatest leadership blessing God put in place: community.

This is the challenge for missional organizational cultures: What is the special flavor, the saltiness we are to manifest as communities into the world? If our cultures are just as flawed as those in the secular sector, what makes us uniquely qualified for our missional work? Shouldn't we just close shop and go work for the bigger and better resourced organizations across town?

Our saltiness is the love we have for one another. As John writes, "Let me give you a new command: Love one another. In the same way I loved you, you love one another. This is how everyone will recognize that you are my disciples—when they see the love you have for each other" (John 13:34-35 *The Message*). If we claim to be followers of Jesus in our profession and programs, the same should also be true in our shared relationships, manifested by our love as sisters and brothers.

POSTSCRIPT

Healthy relationships can sometimes transform into consensual romantic relationships in the workplace between single staff members. This is something to celebrate. It can be difficult to meet a partner in today's complex society, and the organization can offer opportunities for like-minded people on the same path to explore a relationship. Most organizations have policies in place to accommodate this. The culture of the organization should do the same. It is not a nuisance; it's a joy.

● ● ●

A belonging organization pursuing a healthy culture

- has robust policies and processes in place to protect the safety of all staff and clients from sexual exploitation and abuse,
- defines for itself "good leadership" and persistently expects it from all people entering leadership roles (even previously untouchable senior leaders),
- embraces both feminine and masculine leadership qualities and knows that the leadership table is incomplete without both present,
- and creates community between women and men in healthy ways; avoids creating spaces that exclude women.

CHAPTER SIX

HUMAN RESOURCES FOR CULTURES OF BELONGING

Human resources is rarely recognized for what it could be—the strategic driver of how employees experience the culture of an organization. If executives allocated half the energy they dedicate to managing difficult star employees to equitable routine policies and practices, our organizations would be healthier, employees would be happier, and we would see better organizational performance. HR policies and practices are not a bother or irrelevant. They are at the very heart of ensuring a healthy, equitable organizational culture.

Consider a former colleague, Kristen, who graduated summa cum laude with her bachelor's degree in English. During her studies she spent summers interning in nonprofit work overseas, first in Africa then in Latin America, and after graduation she felt like she'd hit the jackpot when she landed a junior role at an international nonprofit.

Shortly after arriving at the organization, she realized something was amiss. Despite weekly devotionals and the passion her team shared about the people they served, the culture felt off. Team meetings quickly grew heated, and more than once she witnessed leaders shouting at each other. Management huddled in offices talking behind each other's backs. Her boss was fired shortly after she came on, but no one ever explained the reason why. There were just a lot of rumors. The place felt toxic and unruly.

After ten disappointing months Kristen decided to leave the organization. "It's not that I thought it wouldn't be messy. I mean, it's people, and people are messy," she later told us. "I was just shocked at how disconnected what we were trying to do on the outside felt to how we treated each other on the inside. It was like two totally different organizations."

Kristen's story, or a version of it, is painfully familiar to many working in the missional space. The utmost parameters of what the organizational culture will allow—in this case backbiting, fighting, and immature leadership behaviors—end up becoming the norm, not the exception. On the contrary, organizations that have the discipline to expect good leadership and employee behaviors from their people can create a culture that manifests the mission on the inside of the organization.

At its core, human resource work is culture work. It establishes the boundaries of what the organization will and will not tolerate. When organizations create explicit and implicit rules of engagement for everyone, morale and productivity levels increase. Employees also experience higher levels of suitability and purpose when they feel aligned with the values of the organization and when those values are fairly communicated through enacted policies and practices.

This isn't just a women's issue. According to a Women in the Workplace Study, gender alone does not explain attrition. Men and women leave or desire to stay in organizations at the same rate, and addressing organizational culture at the policy and practice level becomes a game-changer for both men and women equally.

Missional organizations walk timidly in creating their company ethos for fear of overstepping the lines of what their employees define as their personal walk with God. "This isn't my church," we've heard people comment.

"I don't need you to teach me how to make good decisions." So organizations tiptoe around what's acceptable and leave too much to individual leaders and employee discretion. This can result in the following real-life examples we have witnessed and had recounted to us:

- Individuals bring their theological perspectives about men and women in leadership to work. Even if the organization embraces women in leadership on paper, leaders sabotage women's advancement because they disagree with it privately. "She wouldn't be a great fit on our executive team; she challenges ideas a lot and would slow us down," one senior vice president noted to his colleagues when considering a female candidate for promotion.

- Men and women working in the same job are offered different compensation because the man has a family and is a "provider" and the woman is single and "doesn't need all that money."

- Employees refuse to participate in community life because they disagree with elements of the organization's faith expression. Instead, they verbalize opinions against it.

- Male leaders don't have proper guidance on how to engage with female staff. They can either avoid women, thus refusing them opportunities to advance, or make inappropriate advances toward them. In a few missional organizations, women shared that their bosses refused to have one-on-one meetings with them, citing the Billy Graham rule. As a result, the men on the team received better-quality feedback and stretch assignments.

- Guidance on everyday work activities (remote work, travel, sick leave) is formulated at the discretion of individual managers. Whether your manager is "cool" or "uncool" ends up determining the employee experience across the organization.

You don't have to work at culture—and many organizations choose not to—but it's imprudent to think that decision doesn't have a cost, whether explicit or implicit. A nondecision is a decision. And like the old saying goes, the culture of your organization "eats strategy for breakfast." Every single time. So here is the invitation: If our organization is trying to become a place that is welcoming to diverse employees and leaders, what do we need to change about the culture that exists today to create a culture of belonging? Let's look at the paradigm shift we need in human resource practices and policies, from throwing the recruiting net, to determining who gets praise and promotion, to celebrating retirement and all the stages in between.

HIRING FOR CULTURES OF BELONGING

Job post wording can deter the qualified female candidates organizations are looking to recruit. Research shows that male- or female-gendered wording in job advertisements can discourage applicants of the opposite gender. If, based on how an ad is worded, a candidate feels they "wouldn't belong," even if they're qualified, they are unlikely to apply. It's the perception about belonging, rather than actual qualifications, that deters candidates. Words matter. Terms like "ambitious," "assertive," "dominate," "ninja" (please don't use "ninja"), and "takes risks" have been found to be off-putting to women. In faith-based organizations, phrases like "experience in pastoral leadership" lead the mind to envision the majority of pastors who are men, which deters women from applying.

Mine your internal talent before posting the role externally. Often organizations overlook the wealth of experience within their walls because staff are pigeonholed in their defined roles and many people remain unaware of team members' past professional experiences. What if your recruiters first headhunted from within the organization? One major nonprofit recently named a CEO who started with them as an intern a few decades earlier. Publicize about recruiting from the inside. Another organization uses a database, something akin to an internal LinkedIn, that allows recruiters and managers to quickly search for existing staff who have certain skills, certifications, and other experiences they may have brought to the organization even if their current role doesn't use them.

Use a résumé "scrubbing" service. The best candidates may be eliminated by the initial résumé review due to unconscious bias against women or men in a certain role. Removing gender and cultural identifiers like gender, race, and age from applications will result in a higher percentage—upward of

25 percent—of diverse candidates brought forward for interviewing. A blind review of résumés gives all candidates a fair chance of making it to the next round based on merit. At the very least, hiding names reduces unconscious bias when selecting candidates to interview.

A colleague who recently participated in country director panels describes reviewing writing samples without identifiers: "As I was reviewing, I was focused solely on the quality of the response along with their writing ability, which was a key consideration for the role. It was liberating to not consider personalities or specific individuals at that stage of selection, only skills."

Establish an interview panel to avoid individual bias in hiring. A study on hiring as cultural matching found that individual hiring managers actually made decisions in a way that closely resembled selecting friends or romantic partners. Concerns about absolute productivity were overshadowed by cultural similarities like leisure pursuits, life experiences, and self-presentation styles. Alternatively, having a 360-degree view of the candidate from multiple participants on an interviewing panel should provide insights into the candidate and their qualifications for the role, reducing individual bias and establishing the credibility of the new hire given that their credentials and experience will have been vetted by multiple colleagues in the organization. This practice should be routine at least for senior leadership interviews but, to the extent possible, should also become a hiring norm across the enterprise.

Predetermined interview questions and a scoring rubric that prioritizes key elements of the role create an interview process with effectiveness, fairness, consistency, and legal protection built in. Interview situations are littered with traps like beauty bias (yes, we are more likely to hire someone who is attractive to us than not), similar-to-me-bias, or the halo effect ("You went to *Harvard*?"). Using predetermined questions, including set evaluation criteria, can decrease natural gut reactions in an interview situation. Some leaders take great pride in letting their gut guide their decisions. To that we say they need to have a pretty infallible and well-documented track record of their gut decisions. Otherwise, everyone should use the tools that are available.

As noted above, an individual hiring manager decision can bring significant unconscious bias into the process. Consider a manager with an unwelcome management style—let's say a sarcastic or snarky manner of communication. If the hiring process is not clearly defined at an organizational level, the manager is likely to hire people with similar styles, replicating the unwanted behavior.

Managers who are intentional about creating cultures of belonging understand that they're not hiring a friend. Instead, they know they don't always have to agree with a person on their team. They know how to be quiet and listen when a team member knows better or disagrees with them. They have the ability to admit when they make a mistake or work it out when their team member does the same. If these conditions are in place, managers can hire the *best* candidate. Establishing the rubric and standard questions by which each candidate is assessed, as well as reporting results and notes to HR, establishes practices that can minimize unintended bias in recruiting and hiring for a better organizational culture.

WELCOMING PEOPLE IN

Transparency around rank and salary range is a best practice when welcoming new staff. While it is common for an organization to try to "get the best for less" when it comes to talent, inevitably it becomes a significant demotivator when people learn they're being grossly underpaid and underranked when those elements aren't transparent during the hiring process. And employees do find out. We foresee a future where nonprofits are required to make this type of data public through agencies such as Charity Navigator or other best practices–monitoring organizations. And demonstrating gender parity in pay will go a long way toward attracting the best talent.

This same transparency is required during onboarding so that candidates know there might be limitations to advancing into leadership roles because of their gender. Organizations don't want to advertise this because it is not "politically correct" in the secular space, but the reality is there are ceilings for women in certain organizations. Some don't allow women to be national directors. Others may technically "allow" women in senior roles but have never placed a woman in such a position in the past—aspiring women have a right to know this unspoken practice before they invest their talents in the organization.

We encourage all women to ask these questions during the interview process so they can make an informed decision as to whether the organization will be a place where they can fully thrive. And don't just ask if there are opportunities for women to lead—ask for present titles of women in leadership roles.

As organizations work to become more welcoming to underrepresented groups, one promising practice has been the creation of affinity groups. Though it may seem counterintuitive to create a more inclusive organization by sectioning off employees by gender, race, or other affinity identifiers, having safe spaces to connect, ask questions, and feel welcomed and comfortable can go a long way toward a more successful onboarding into the organization, which will inevitably feel strange to them during the first weeks and months.

In fact, the smart organization knows that these early employees are also the best group to hear from when it comes to describing what the organizational culture is like. They're new and fresh, and they haven't been "swimming in the water" long. They can tell you a great deal about how the culture feels to those experiencing it for the first time.

DEFINING AND MEASURING PERFORMANCE

A focus on belonging does not exclude expectations of high performance but rather zooms in on the essentials. It takes a project-based approach to work, which allows people to decide when, where, and how they work. This approach puts the onus on leaders: What are they asking their people to do and how are they measuring excellent performance? When these questions are answered, team members have clarity and transparency on the *what* while they can focus on the *how* with more flexibility.

When it comes to performance evaluations, trusting in our unbiased opinions and feelings about a person doesn't provide the organization with a system of parity and fairness—instead we should rely on data. How we personally feel about someone does not provide us as managers with adequate information to evaluate their performance as good or bad—especially compared to other team members. We recommend using systems like objectives and key results (OKRs) or key performance indicators (KPIs), or really any system that provides managers with objective data on success and moves us away from subjective and unfair evaluations on individual performance. These offer a good option that merges achievement scales and metrics with an ongoing dialogue about goals that have been agreed on by both team member and supervisor. Self-evaluation and self-rating are not always useful: women tend to underestimate their performance, whereas men tend to overestimate theirs. If self-evaluation is used, team members should provide specific examples and data to back up their rating.

Based on research, women specifically benefit from real-time feedback on an almost weekly basis. Part of the intentional development of leaders in an organization is to help every supervisor understand their role as coach and ensure they are coaching women on their team as intentionally as the men. In general, performance feedback should be ongoing and the relationship between manager and team member so open that it is addressed on a routine basis. A useful approach is to make feedback a two-way street, where team members are also allowed to give feedback to the manager. Of course, this assumes the manager is a healthy, low-ego leader who doesn't hold grudges or practice retaliation. Certain managers are afraid of providing timely and constructive feedback, but this is exactly what women benefit from the most. When feedback is real time and uses examples of specific behaviors and situations, team members can course-correct in real time, minimizing continued conflict and unwanted behavior.

A mechanism should be in place to challenge or ask for a re-review of performance if an employee disagrees with how they are rated. This will move the conversation into the documented realm, including the specific metrics by which the review was conducted, and highlight any biased subjectivity that was used.

As the saying goes, it's hard to hit a bull's-eye if you can't see the target. It's hard for both women and men to succeed in their work if success is undefined. The criteria of what constitutes poor, good, and excellent performance should be instituted and shared openly. Managers need to be explicit about what they want and resource their people adequately. Are they supported?

Do they have needs for time or resources? Are *you* providing them with the support they need to hit the bull's-eye?

ADVANCING IN THE ORGANIZATION

Decisions about who gets developed in your organization start with identifying who you'd like to see expand their portfolio and influence. When we interviewed senior male leaders on what the women under them needed to do to advance, we heard responses like these:

- "She hasn't had enough time in the deep end of the pool yet."
- "She hasn't had enough executive seasoning."
- "She needs to be more assertive in meetings."

You can see where this is going. It becomes a Catch-22 when women aren't developed for executive-level positions because they haven't had the opportunity for executive-level experience or when their leadership style is critiqued and discounted through a lens of traditional masculine leadership qualities. The "lacking experience" argument also ignores the reality that someone at some point in these executives' own career took a chance on them and pushed them into the deep end of the pool . . . and then stayed close to ensure they didn't drown.

Identifying high-potential staff, creating succession plans, and fast-tracking employees for development are all potentially biased processes if we aren't mindful and intentional. We firmly believe that professional growth training should be available far and wide within the organization, even extending to the community leaders and communities we serve.

At some point, though, organizations need to be intentional about identifying and developing those who have exhibited high potential and creating succession plans for senior leaders. What leadership qualities are being used to determine this? Are they the old standard criteria of "the ones who get lots done" or the "yes men" of the organization? Those won't be the high-potential staff and successors who help you create a new, better-performing culture.

Promotions are often based on subjective measures. Discussions around performance of leaders are diluted by preferences, politics, and management ideology. When it comes to promotions, perceptions still trump reality.

Recently a leader of a large nonprofit described the selection of a new vice president with, "The chosen candidate showed up as confident, self-assured, strategic-minded, and had experiences that were just a bit better than the other candidates." In this case, the other three candidates were women who had already held senior positions for larger organizations. What often inches one candidate over another is a predetermined set of attributes we look for in leaders, and those attributes often look like our own rather than consideration for what the health of our organization needs.

The practice of aligning candidates with culture-of-belonging criteria and making those decisions public will challenge natural knee-jerk decisions based on gut instinct. Selection panels should be able to articulate how the selected candidate will work to make the shared culture better—how will she or he enhance the culture? What if our criteria included how well candidates had formed and developed diverse people on their teams? What if criteria included the oft-dismissed leadership qualities of listening, empathy, and collaboration rather than the individualistic characteristics often labeled as "strong leadership"? Even better, if our organizations are truly about cultivating whole persons for kingdom work, what if we sought appropriate input from a candidate's inner circle when assessing their emotional health and spiritual maturity for leadership roles? If we want to change the toxic workaholic culture of our organizations, wouldn't assessing the healthy, whole-life practices of caring for spouses and children speak volumes about what kind of leader that person would be inside our organization?

SENIOR LEADERSHIP PROMOTIONS AND SUCCESSION PLANNING

If we asked most people in an organization, "Do you know how various leaders get targeted for senior roles and succession plans?" they wouldn't be able to articulate the exact formula. That's because most organizations don't have a strategy around this. It's very subjective and left to individual managers to determine "fit," sometimes creating their own performance criteria or simply rewarding the staff they get along with best or who work the longest hours.

The 2019 Women in the Workplace Study states that in corporate America, progress at the top is constrained by a "broken rung." The biggest obstacle to senior management is the promotion of women to first-tier management roles; only seventy-two women are promoted to leadership for every hundred men. If companies hire and promote women as first-level managers at the same rate as men, we will add a million women to management in the next five years. However, there are simply too few women in the pipeline to advance. Any organization that runs a report on gender and leadership by job level will see the severe decline in the number of women when a certain level of leadership is reached.

Setting organizational targets is still double-edged. A woman will experience backlash if colleagues and leaders feel she was promoted simply on the basis of a company-set target on their gender. Yet men are promoted simply based on their gender *all the time,* and there is never any backlash. If companies are serious about fixing the pipeline, aggressive initial targets at the management level are a key option—one that has been found in many organizations and governments to be the catalyst to creating more diverse cultures. This doesn't mean the creation or continuation of a quota system, but organizations must establish some baseline target for what "diverse culture" means to them.

Additionally, it makes sense to aggressively focus on female talent in divisions where female talent is not usually prevalent. Human resources, marketing, and program support routinely have women working at all levels. Targets should be set in program leadership, strategy and operations, and finance, where women are almost entirely missing and from where leaders rise into roles of CEO and president. Ensuring women opportunities to lead in the most central and visible roles in the organization will in turn secure a future leadership pipeline of qualified women candidates.

High-potential female staff are often overlooked in the promotion process, as one study notes: "Entry-level women are 18% less likely to receive promotions than are their male colleagues." And executive succession plans, if they exist, continue to pull male colleagues up rather than evaluating a diverse list of candidates and providing intentional coaching and mentoring of both women and men.

Even great promotion and succession-planning tools like the 9-Box, if not used properly, can bias results. The 9-Box gathers a group around nine boxes, with candidate labels ranging from "talent risk" to "consistent star." The process rates candidates across a range, from low to moderate to high, on two axes: the candidate's potential and the candidate's performance. Kudos to this method for trying to fix the problem of women being judged only on past performance and men being judged mostly on future potential. However, depending on how you execute this process, you can still end up with slanted rankings.

Simple steps to improve the 9-Box discussion process and reduce inherent bias and favoritism include: a) ensuring each rater knows the candidates they are evaluating and knows them well, b) ensuring each has had significant, not just cursory, work involvement with that candidate, and c) ensuring diversity among the 9-Box raters to hear differing perspectives on each candidate.

Organizations that require the submission and tracking of every supervisor's high-potential staff list and succession plan are able to spot glaring leanings toward homogenous candidate pools and remedy them. This includes acknowledging and rewarding leaders who ensure they are cultivating a diverse group of talent for the future. This requires intentionality, but it is not difficult.

WHAT DOES EMPLOYEE WELL-BEING REALLY MEAN?

The experience of a global pandemic was the impetus for a focus on new organizational performance metrics—how well our employees are coping. Sad, really, that it takes such a devastating global experience to return us to humanity. Organizations were forced to get creative and flexible in what got accomplished and how. Now that we've all had a taste of a different way of working, the majority of workers don't want to return to their old ways. The corporate sector has been playing with different ideas of how to care for employees better, testing everything from relaxation pods to game rooms at work. But rather than turning to these novelties, what if we changed the way we looked at performance so that well-being could be accomplished based on individual needs?

Earlier we noted that if we looked at performance from an outcomes-based approach, we would move away from measuring high performance based on hours spent at the office or measuring commitment based on how available someone is over their weekend and during their evenings. Each of us knows the work we need to accomplish and what it takes to achieve our best energy and best thinking.

For me (Beth), my longtime mantra is, "Nothing godly happens before 10 a.m." I love the flexibility to work 10 to 7—these are my most energetic hours, and they allow me to have a morning routine I love (dog walk, me walk/workout, breakfast, devotional, meditation). I know for Eeva, 5:30 a.m. is the best time to tackle big projects before her family is up, while her head is still clear, and before the day's mass of emails starts accumulating.

Training managers to manage with flexibility based on what their staff members need and how they work best will improve employee engagement and result in a better product for the organization. There can still be times in the day when everyone is needed, but this approach puts an end to the notorious meeting string that starts at 8 a.m. every day, ends at 6 p.m. every night, and pushes deep work into evenings and weekends.

This way of thinking allows conversations around bigger questions, such as: Do we really need all these meetings? What are the merits of a four-day workweek, as some countries are testing out? Do we spend enough time developing and empowering our managers to lead their teams in the best way for the members? Let's take this moment in history to rethink all aspects of work to change the culture for everyone's well-being.

POLICIES THAT WELCOME WOMEN'S BODIES

Expanding organizations for women's participation and contributions means creating policies and practices that invite women as full individuals. It means making sure the employee experience welcomes a woman's whole being, including her body. Decades of effort and resources have gone into building policies and frameworks that do not acknowledge women as central in the workplace. Considerable intentional effort and resources are needed to rebuild structures and policies that welcome women as whole human beings.

Maternal and parental leave. The United States is among a handful of countries that do not offer women and families a federally mandated maternal and parental leave. This is outrageous. Our capitalist ideology prefers that care work be free, and if women can continue to be convinced by the media, churches, leadership, and each other that this is the work they are best suited for, the problem will take care of itself. Organizations that care for families and female employees must step up to the plate and make sure they have a generous parental leave or, at minimum, maternity leave. Parental leave enables couples to decide who will stay home based on income and career goals. It also enables both parents to share an initial bonding time with the baby.

Just as we serve children of the world as missional organizations, so we must care for the children of our own staff.

But having the policy isn't enough. Too many men forgo their paternity leave because they fear it removes them from the leadership track. Again, how can we be organizations working for the good of healthy kids and families around the world but not require the men on our staff to start their own kids off with healthy bonding time with dad? Having a leave policy isn't enough. We need a culture where taking the leave is not only acceptable but also encouraged and celebrated.

Returning to work after having a baby. Beyond leave, the return to work for new mothers needs special attention. Beginning with a part-time schedule on return may make the new balancing of work and childcare more attainable. The thought of a daily 8 a.m. return three months after giving birth is daunting to the strongest of worker bees. We've heard leadership comments like, "She used to be such a producer before she had a baby."

Let's take a time-out here.

A woman's physical body is barely healed after three months, let alone the emotional and psychological impacts of giving birth and becoming a new mom. This is not nothing. Women and men need individualized support and solutions after the birth of a child so they can assess the needs of the baby (which vary and can be unexpected), as well as their own. In this stage a new parent's job performance may fluctuate—tasks that were attainable on a full night's sleep may prove challenging on half that. During this important season many male executives may have avoided having any responsibility, and their wives carried the burden alone. The next generation of dads is looking to change that.

Nursing and nursing rooms. Many missional organizations work on global and US-based health projects. Those of us doing this work know the benefits of breastfeeding for the first six months of a baby's life. A hundred things can go awry as new mothers and newborn babies figure out the synchrony of breastfeeding. It is a fragile and challenging time in a mother's life. Flexibility, sensitivity, and awareness are key postures for leaders working with new mothers in the workplace. Just as we are anxious to see babies flourish in the communities we serve, with well-nourished bodies and round cheeks, so we must celebrate the same among staff. When it comes to facilities, organizations should offer new mothers the space to pump breast milk in a private and hygienic environment, as well as store it and clean their equipment.

Flexible work schedules and telework. It's not just parents who are looking for policies that support fluctuations in personal lives. Employees who care for elderly parents or other relatives need the same consideration, as do team members who are working on graduate degrees or other important goals. Flexible work schedules and telework are key in improving employee satisfaction across the board, not to mention a totally effective way to work. An outdated leadership model depends on the need to *see* and *supervise* people's work. Flexible work assumes that people are adults and know how to self-supervise. The role of supervisor is to monitor quality and timeliness of work products rather than rely on the old "butt in chair" expectation. This requires supervisors to set priorities for their members toward shared goals. It takes more focus and foresight to lead people this way. If the Covid-19 pandemic taught us anything, it is that when you have people you trust and who are committed to the mission, work will get done from literally anywhere. We hope missional organizations recognize the opportunity of this moment as many in the private sector have: we are no longer limited to recruiting people who can make a cross-country move to our organizations but can join our ranks from anywhere.

Menstruation. Menstruation is a health topic that some organizations are starting to address. While in the Western context female staff have resources and access to running water, the same may not apply to global staff. This is an awkward topic, as expressed by a male colleague from a global office: "As a supervisor, there are certain 'women's health issues' that are uncomfortable to be shared between genders—because of this discomfort we would rather assemble a male leadership team."

Yes, you read that right.

Menstruation, access to adequate hygiene resources, and women's privacy are public health concerns many organizations tackle with their WASH (water, sanitation, hygiene) programming. Hundreds of thousands of girls drop out of school every year at puberty because of the stigma related to their period. Let's hope we can do better for our own staff and be responsive to contextual needs as they arise.

Travel. Leaders may end up passing on a woman with small children or the possibility of pregnancy for leadership roles that require travel because they assume the woman herself is not interested. More farsighted organizations explore options for leaders with young children to continue in impactful roles. A senior scientist working for a leading university continued her work and travel and frequently brought along her daughter because the university policy allowed for this. It was a nominal expense for the institution but a huge benefit for the still nursing mother. Another exemplary NGO provided onsite childcare so moms with new babies could attend leadership training and have their infant looked after in the conference room next door and visit with their baby on breaks. This is the kind of creativity being deployed by organizations that are serious about "making it work." Equally, opportunities should be considered for dads who are looking for opportunities to spend time with their children, whether through travel allowances or through greater flexibility when their wife is traveling.

RELEASING OUR PEOPLE WELL

The way people exit an organization speaks volumes. Even though the missional sector's attrition rates fluctuate between a sky-high 20 and 25 percent, we don't know how to part ways with our people well.

The famous quote "Hire slow; fire fast" is not just a platitude. For the reasons we've laid out in this chapter, taking your time with recruiting allows for interview panels and a cross section of staff to interact with the candidate. We should take the time we need; our people's well-being and the culture depend on it. On the other hand, when someone is not working out, it's not usually known only to the supervisor; it's known to the rest of the team, and it's usually known to the individual. Often the greatest act of stewardship we can undertake is releasing a person who is not performing or flourishing in the organization as quickly as possible. Months spent in flux harms team morale and production and often paralyzes the team member from contributing in meaningful ways.

HR provides us with tools to communicate with people about their performance. Ninety-day reviews, annual reviews, performance improvement plans, and continuous conversation between employee and supervisor allow for transparency in the relationship between team member and leader. We have a "good Christian" syndrome of avoiding difficult performance evaluations. Yet we are called on to "speak the truth in love," as sisters and brothers.

When it is time for a person to leave your organization, release them. This can be a celebration or a lament. Leaders often hide circumstances. Hours are spent communicating behind closed doors about why a person didn't work out. Why don't we take half that energy and release people well by hearing them (no matter how painful their experience) and honoring and supporting them as they prepare for next steps? We *do not* do this well in missional organizations.

"Not a great fit"—the unexplained exits of strong women. The concept of "fit" is problematic when the definition of who fits and who doesn't is determined by a monocultured, monogendered leadership team. Organizations obviously have a bigger problem than just hiring, as we have watched many, many women executives get hired into missional organizations over the last ten years and then "exit" within a short period of time.

When this happened six times in an eighteen-month window in one organization, we decided to ask why.

In interviews with each of these women leaders and looking at the profile of the group, we found commonalities: every woman had an accomplished career, was credentialed in her field, and exhibited a healthy confidence in her calling and work. They all assumed a level of equality within the organization and felt free to speak from their expertise and lend their insights. All were stunned initially and then repeatedly when they received admonishments for being too vocal, for not "falling into line," and for garnering too much positive attention among employees.

The remedy? Senior male leaders began finding reasons why these women weren't a "good fit" and ultimately let each one go with a hefty severance package tied to a nondisclosure agreement. This way their pattern of silencing strong women, each of whom could have been a consideration for CEO, would not come to light.

Women support one another, and the sector will eventually identify which organizations engage in this kind of treatment and which ones don't. A movement is afoot in other industries to do away with nondisclosure agreements. For too long they have been the tool of bad actors to silence people from telling their truth and leaving toxic leadership in place. But aren't they even more offensive in missional organizations where truth, transparency, and honesty are biblical values? Leaders need to think long and hard as they reach for the "not a great fit" excuse and ask themselves, "Who defined 'fit' in the first place?"

How long is too long—leadership tenure. A question that is asked often in missional organizations is how long a senior leader should remain in the role. There are a few competing philosophies on this. In the corporate world, turnover happens more frequently, in part because of clear metrics for determining success (increases or decreases in revenues, profits, stock prices, and so on). In the nonprofit sector there are at least five different ways by which organizational effectiveness is measured. This, coupled with the presence of board members who potentially don't understand the development sector or use "he's such a nice guy" metrics to judge success, puts an organization at risk of mediocre performance and keeping toxic leadership in place for a long time. This reality makes it difficult for anyone in the organization to advance, let alone those who are not presumed to be senior leadership material.

We have observed that somewhere around the eight-to-ten-year mark, leaders go from acting like stewards of their role and the organization to owners of their role and the organization, and that is a dangerous transition to make. The organization can fall into a cult of personality and start to believe that the leader is "irreplaceable." Long-tenured leaders can also become too firmly entrenched in their own notion of "who fits," or what ideas will work and what won't, based on outdated experience. A bad idea a decade ago isn't necessarily a bad idea today.

While a controversial move, we advocate for organizations utilizing job rotations and term limits on senior leader roles. This opens up executive seats to new voices. It allows current leaders to stay fresh and not fall into the traps of ownership that can squash the very innovation the missional sector so desperately needs.

AN ORGANIZATION WHERE ALL CAN BELONG

Sustainability is one of the most important goals of a development program. If we eventually leave the community and the systems that have been put in place break down—the water pumps rust and stop working, the church networks stop meeting, mothers in the community stop seeking safe delivery services—we consider this a failure. Yet sustainability is rarely a metric of our organizational culture work. Just as we look for communities to thrive *out there*, a belonging organization looks for people to thrive inside the organization, both now and in the future. In a belonging culture leaders desire to leave people and organizations better than how they found them.

Based on our definition, belonging organizations are committed to the acceptance and well-being of all employees, regardless of gender, race, or age. This commitment fosters connections and maintains lasting, positive, encouraging relationships among diverse team members. A culture of belonging thus embraces employees in all stages of life and works with individuals to make their participation in the organization sustainable and enjoyable. If you're interpreting this focus as a "feel-good, hippy-dippy" value where everyone just does what feels good to them, nothing could be further from the truth.

Cultures of belonging look for people who have a demonstrated record of valuing diversity, encouraging discussion, and drawing out different viewpoints. People who are missional are not limited to one profile. They are the unique, gifted women and men all around us who desire to see the good work of our organizations realized.

Organizations that invest in belonging

- ensure that time and resources are invested toward increasing gender diversity through hiring, promotion, retention, and targeted development of women for leadership roles,

- move from thinking of staff as "culture fit" and look for people who are "culture add,"

- and challenge standing norms on leadership tenures and have plans in place to give new, diverse leaders opportunities to learn and lead.

CHAPTER SEVEN

DEVELOPING PEOPLE FOR CULTURES OF BELONGING

The "complete leader" is a myth. There is no magical list of competencies and skills we can intentionally develop to ensure every leader is the complete package. So why do we keep looking for complete leader unicorns?

When we have the courage to recognize our flaws and the areas where we need help from others, we can release tasks, responsibility, and platform to others' expertise, vision, ideas, and inputs. As followers of Jesus, we are called to the freedom to release perfectionism, being all-knowing and all-capable. By allowing for incompleteness in ourselves, we can also welcome it in others. The complete package is created in community, when incomplete people recognize that others bring what they themselves don't.

Because of this, every member of an organization's staff needs to grow in key areas that affect shared culture. Recent research has focused on such concepts as character development, ethical

behavior, and empathy as key pathways toward creating a culture of belonging.

THE TRAINING WE ALL NEED

Before there can be successful leadership formation in a missional organization, there are areas of essential formation that apply to all staff.

A shared understanding of the organization's position on theology of genders. In chapter three we discussed the importance of organizations having a public theological or policy statement on gender. In the examples we shared, many organizations expand a theological statement of inclusion to minoritized populations. It's not enough to simply make a statement; it's important for organizations and senior leaders in particular to regularly clarify their theological position on women's leadership. This happens through regular training of all staff, including during new staff orientation, on the organizational stance on gender and diversity at large.

Character development. Since the #MeToo movement, studies have shown that character and ethics training helps organizations address sexism and sexual harassment. Schools and universities used to routinely require courses on character and ethics—perhaps it's time to return to these essential values. Numerous gender allies who shared their stories with us discussed their need to "do what was right" in standing up and advocating for women. This is not the norm, however. Many women we interviewed shared blatant examples of men who lacked character. They spoke of men who promised to be sponsors of women into leadership roles but didn't follow through. We heard stories of colleagues who convinced them to take stretch assignments with promises of promotions and then did not keep that promise, all the while benefiting from the extra hard work women offered. There is an assumption that people of faith serving in missional organizations are people of character, but everyone benefits when basic rules of conduct are shared and understood.

Empathy. Empathy asks the question, What does it take to fully understand the other? Walk two moons in their moccasins. See the organization through their eyes. Hear their story. These simple things can help us develop empathy. Any work in the justice space requires us to feel empathy toward those we're serving—it deepens commitment and keeps us committed when the going gets tough. The same is true inside organizations. If we continue to stay removed from the other in our organizations, we will not understand their story or identify with them through shared experiences.

Belinda Bauman has created a useful framework for developing empathy. Many of the skills within the framework—humanizing the other, listening to and checking your perceptions about the other, and peacemaking—are areas worth exploring and developing for organizations. Missional organizations attract people who feel sympathy toward the poor our organizations serve. What we need is a "closer walk" of empathy with the ones we serve and with those we serve alongside. "The way of empathy chooses to make itself vulnerable by connecting with something deep inside that knows those same feelings of pain, sadness, and fear. . . . Empathy takes the responsibility to know what the other is feeling and is marked by compassion and connection," Bauman states.

Listening. Craig, a senior leader of a missional organization in South Africa, shares his own lessons and efforts to be a better listener. He's tried to develop a habit of hearing others first. As a White male in predominantly Black South Africa, where women suffer significant violence and marginalization every day, he makes a point of not speaking in meetings until a person of color or a woman has spoken. He has consciously chosen to *not* be the first person to speak. Because he is a leader, he is regularly asked to be the first to speak, but he resists, stating, "I'd really like to listen for a while if that's okay."

The listening we speak of here is not distracted listening as we scan computer screens or complete to-do lists while the other person is talking. And it's not faking and going through the motions—nodding your head, uttering the occasional uh-huh, leaning in to display interest. No, deep listening starts with the heart. It starts with a sense of curiosity and desire to understand the other person. And yes, then all those skills—a listening posture, rephrasing what you heard, and affirming nods—become essential and hopefully natural.

The organizational experience is different for women than it is for men. It's sometimes difficult for women to articulate their experience, but it often involves being in meetings and not being heard or offering a profound idea that goes ignored until it comes out of the mouth of the man next to them.

It can feel surreal, dehumanizing, infuriating. We have been conditioned to value male voices and respond well to masculine leadership qualities of assertiveness and confidence in meetings, and these make it hard for many to hear women. Ours will never become a culture of belonging if men and women in the organization cannot hear each other.

Many organizations have begun to set up intentional listening sessions. Initially, and in a way this may seem counterintuitive, as those discussions may need to take place among segregated groups, men with men, women with women. Under existing cultural norms, integrated groups may be unable to share authentically, fear career retribution, or experience a pull to conform to the dominant group's way of communicating. Women-only discussions hold up a mirror to the organizational reality they experience. Women's togetherness helps them say, "No, you aren't crazy. I've felt that too."

Bias awareness. In the words of a beloved male leader, "I know two things about bias—I have blind spots and I don't know what they are." Gender bias is held by women and men alike. We are all socialized in the way we view masculine and feminine attributes and behaviors by the time we are just seven years old. In those early years, the roles our parents and family members filled, the media we were exposed to, and tasks we saw men and women performing in society all shaped how we would view male and female behavior for the rest of our lives. Maybe we learned that men are assertive, strong, and born leaders, just as we learned that women are pleasant, sensitive, and naturally born supporters to men. Those first impressions and socializations have significant implications for our ability to develop a culture where women and men can thrive equally.

One group of researchers concluded,

> The mismatch between qualities attributed to women and qualities thought necessary for leadership places women leaders in a double bind and subjects them to a double standard. Women in positions of authority are thought to be too aggressive or not aggressive enough, and what appears assertive, self-confident, or entrepreneurial in a man often looks abrasive, arrogant, or self-promoting in a woman. . . . By the same token, when women performing traditionally male roles are seen as conforming to feminine stereotypes, they tend to be liked but

not respected, they are judged too soft, emotional, and unassertive to make tough decisions and to come across as sufficiently authoritative.

If organizations and leaders have a bias toward believing men are the only ones who should lead, they will continue to pour more resources into men's development, with promotions, key projects, stretch assignments, and leadership training all focused on promoting masculine leadership styles.

Bias awareness training is one of the most common forms of training organizations are implementing as they make efforts to become more diverse. When implemented well, as part of a larger strategy, bias awareness training can help men and women learn how to recognize partiality and develop a shared language to identify and call it out. It is not the only step, however, and implemented incorrectly, it can increase frustration felt inside an organization. Recognizing bias doesn't solve everything. Awareness of bias alone doesn't help organizations develop a sense of belonging. For that, leaders must commit to transparency on how bias training will improve decision making.

Coaching and difficult conversations. As a rule, people aren't good at giving good coaching feedback and are extraordinarily bad at providing constructive criticism. It seems most of us avoid uncomfortable conversations at any cost, even to our own detriment. If organizations view mistakes and imperfection as unacceptable or an immediate cause for demotion, firing, or marginalization, it's understandable why people are hesitant to give and receive negative feedback. But if the organization sees failures and mistakes as part of learning and growing, not to mention innovation and creativity, getting good at constructive feedback is essential for the organization to thrive.

Leaders must grow comfortable with the uncomfortable. We easily replace true relationships with superficiality, exacerbated by pseudo-communities such as Facebook and LinkedIn and the safe distance they provide us. True community means having conversations about uncomfortable things, including differences, biases, hurtful words or behaviors, confusion over gender sensitivities, cultural differences, and differing ways of working and thinking. Many men are afraid of saying the wrong thing to or about female colleagues or that what they are saying could be misunderstood. Women too are often unwilling to speak up about the comments and behaviors they experience on a regular basis. These conversations may require outside facilitation until pressing into the uncomfortable becomes more common and difficult conversations become the norm.

Inclusion and welcoming. This topic forces us to break away from the zero-sum game we play when it comes to diversity, which says, "If someone else gains, I lose." That's subscribing to a scarcity mentality and doesn't reflect the God of abundance we know and worship. What does inclusion look like? It doesn't mean including everyone in everything to the point of inefficiency. It does mean ensuring diverse voices and perspectives are intentionally sought for key decision making, for strategy development, and for program design. It also helps leaders learn how to welcome alternative views other than their own and not hold on to final decision making in all matters but rather allow consensus to guide the result at times.

Spiritual formation. The thoughtless, hurtful, or divisive behavior we experience inside our organizations stems from spiritual poverty and a marred identity. In his groundbreaking book *Walking with the Poor*, Bryant Myers describes poverty as a consequence of sin. The poverty Myers speaks of reaches far beyond lack of money or resources, into every area of our lives.

While in our missional work we can easily identify poverty among the communities we serve, we are not so quick to see it in our own lives and inside our organizations. But to acknowledge and address poverty in the communities we work alongside, we must first address the poverty in our own lives. God complexes, mistaking work for worship, coveting titles and power, believing in a scarcity theology that tells us that if women advance, men lose out—these are just a few expressions of poverty and marred identity. They point to the need for organizations to be intentional about developing the spiritual health of their staff. This focus on spiritual health is not an effort to replace church or be their pastor but to ensure that in working on the front lines of extreme global poverty, our people will be spiritually equipped and armored to serve.

Focus on spiritual formation is also an invitation for missional organizations to become countercultural. When work cultures in the secular context value overwork, efficiency, and productivity, missional organizations can centralize Sabbath as well as mental, physical, and spiritual health. It takes vulnerability on the part of an organization to remove the worship of work and productivity from the center and replace it with worship of the one who ultimately gives us everything we need to do this good work (2 Peter 1:3). As people of faith, we believe that investing in spiritual formation yields outcomes far beyond a moment in time. One large organization decided decades ago to invest in the spiritual formation of its leadership candidates (half of whom were women). Today, that organization exceeds all others in gender representation on its board, executive team, and team of national directors. Women are flourishing in all levels of the organization.

WHAT WOMEN NEED

What do women need if they are to bring their very best to their daily work? Let's start with what they don't.

Women don't need to be developed to act more like men. Women don't need to be trained to "soften their approach," "exude more confidence," "exude less confidence," or any of the other never-ending mixed messages women receive depending on their organization's culture. Many women reject the idea of an expanded role or senior leadership if it means having to behave like male executives to "fit in."

The intentional development that *is* called for focuses on empowering women to be fully who they are. Our organizations need women to lead from their strengths. A recent McKinsey survey demonstrated that leadership traits displayed by women are "highly applicable to future global challenges." In the absence of clear strategy around what organizations need in order to meet future challenges, we default to the models offered by our current executives—preferring individualistic to participative decision making or control and corrective action to inspiration. Women *and* men need women to lead from their strengths. As women are released to be who they fully are, men are also released.

When I (Beth) coach women, I start by reminding them that they are God's beloved. Stating this simple truth out loud usually brings on tears. Too often life pulls us far away from our first identity—as God's beloved. We get lost in the constant search for affirmation, purpose, and identity from everywhere else. We *are* God's beloved, created in his image, called for his purposes, and gifted for exactly such a time as this. When we come back to this first identity, we are able to put everything else into perspective.

Women need spaces to connect with each other within an organization. We mentioned affinity groups earlier as places where women, especially women of color, can find a safe space to connect and speak with others who are likely to understand their experiences. It comes as a relief to speak with empathetic colleagues who can offer support and encouragement. A group of peers gives people a "space to belong" within the broader organization, which can sometimes feel large and unwelcoming.

Formal and informal groups, however, can also invoke fear in the dominant class of the organization. One interviewee discussed how when she began attending women's leadership lunches, a few male colleagues grew defensive and made comments to the tune of, "What are you plotting over there?" This was likely meant as a joke, but when roles are reversed, all-male gatherings are rarely questioned.

After years of receiving the messages that communicate, "There is something wrong with you and the way you lead," women need to be reaffirmed that they are gifted and wired in unique ways for a reason, just as men are, and their style is much-needed in the organization. Intentional development that helps women uncover and cultivate their natural talents sets them free to be the fierce leaders God designed them to be.

Nancy confesses that after a great deal of learning and reflection on toxic leadership and work culture, she realized the cost of playing the part: "I contribute my upward mobility in the organization to learning to play the game. I learned how to 'act like a woman acting like a man.' Every time I did it, I hurt myself, because I didn't listen to my own voice. I just worried about how I was coming across. If I had focused on what *I* could do to add value, I would have been bigger, brighter, and better."

Shirley states, "It comes down to one very simple thing for women to feel empowered. Just let us make decisions. It's as simple as that. Let us make decisions without having to get your permission or ask for your input. I have a great boss who lets me make decisions regarding my work. Because of this I've seen a huge change in my own confidence in the workplace, my ability to show up in a meeting and speak my mind, because I know she is going to back me up regardless."

Women discover early in male-dominated cultures that they are not encouraged to speak up or speak first. The cost of this muzzling of women cannot be calculated. We can assume that organizations are losing millions of dollars each year by not elevating the voice, thoughts, ideas, strategies, solutions, or innovations of women purely because they have been conditioned to not speak, to speak less, or to defer their ideas to the established leadership in the room.

We are squandering valuable resources.

Women also need coaching that provides a professional sounding board and encouragement to combat the negative self-messaging they've been conditioned to believe. Good coaching inspires women to find ways to demonstrate their leadership skills in their current roles and encourages them to apply for higher-level roles, stretch assignments, or special projects. Stretch assignments and special projects give women the opportunity to sharpen dormant executive skills that have been underutilized in a culture that hasn't appreciated the female executive voice. Good coaching also provides guidance for how to negotiate expanded opportunities.

This type of coaching is not the norm. Research shows that "women get less frequent and lower-quality feedback than men. When people don't receive feedback, they are less likely to know their worth in negotiations. Moreover, people who receive little feedback are ill-equipped to assess their strengths, shore up their weaknesses, and judge their prospects for success and are therefore less able to build the confidence they need to proactively seek promotions or make risky decisions." To bridge this gap, outside coaches are an option, and large organizations can deploy a team of coaches who understand the unique coaching needs of women.

In addition to coaching, executive sponsorship is an effective means of advancing women in an organization. This is different from traditional mentoring. An executive sponsorship is a special relationship "in which the mentor goes beyond giving feedback and advice and uses his or her influence with senior executives to advocate for the mentee," according to *Harvard*

Business Review. "Women are over mentored and under sponsored relative to their male peers and are not advancing in the organization."

Studies show, for example, that "when people are less embedded [in networks], they are also less aware of opportunities for stretch assignments and promotions, and their supervisors may be in the dark about their ambitions. But when women fail to 'lean in' and seek growth opportunities, it is easy to assume that they lack the confidence to do so—not that they lack pertinent information." Sponsors can give access to such networks and information. Most of the women we interviewed for this book mentioned leaders who played the role of a sponsor at one point in their career, advocating for them with positive impacts on their career trajectories.

Sponsor relationships are developed when women have opportunities to spend time with executives to share their backgrounds, career highlights, and future interests. By developing these relationships, senior executives become "spokespeople" in rooms where promotion and advancement discussions are held. "Without sponsorship, a person is likely to be overlooked for promotion, regardless of her competence and performance—particularly at mid-career and beyond, when competition for promotions increases." In most organizations, because there are "more men than women in senior executive positions, the pool of male sponsors at the top is correspondingly larger," states *Harvard Business Review.* "Thus, when left to their own devices, men will be more likely to accrue the advantage of finding a sponsor at the top, someone who looks a lot like them."

Sponsors should also encourage their female colleagues to apply for senior executive roles so they are on leadership's radar for future positions. I (Beth) have coached several female leaders for their interviews for vice presidency positions. Mostly the process included helping women see their skills and abilities and acknowledge how well they were suited for the executive role. This kind of coaching is critical because, again, too many years in a system that leads you to believe you're not worthy of wanting to expand your influence can become a self-fulfilling cycle.

Every significant project a missional organization launches into provides a stretch opportunity for women. Agile teams, global expansions, technology, and program rollouts—these are just a few ways women can gain higher visibility to showcase their leadership abilities while still working in their current positions. When a team is being put together, organizations can be intentional about having women and diverse candidates leading and contributing. Women can be assigned coaches or mentors specific to the initiative. Women can have a platform and ensure their voice is heard when it's time for reporting and presentations. Part of reshaping a culture is the visual representation of women in leadership roles. The more we see it, the more it becomes the accepted cultural norm.

A note of caution, however—there can be a dark side to stretch assignments, as was mentioned by multiple women we interviewed. Julie and Eloise got into a lively conversation about how stretch assignments for women can be used as a means of obtaining free labor and result in work overload. For men and women, stretch assignments start out with the same intent: as opportunities to grow their skills and connect with others outside their normal work role.

Julie comments, "It feels like for men, they get more accolades and rewards for taking on just one or two of these assignments early in their career, and it usually leads to a role expansion or promotion. Women are promised these same things, but assignment after assignment after assignment doesn't result in the same rewards or recognition. It becomes the carrot used to get us to take on the next one."

She concludes, "I'm so tired of being told, 'You just need to get your feet wet with this project before we promote you.' My feet have become waterlogged with all the 'feet wet' projects I've been a part of and promises supervisors have broken." Julie and Eloise agree that this is where having a mentor or coach would be helpful, allowing them to spot this pattern early and enable them to be vocal about desired and agreed-on outcomes.

Finally, a great way to develop women is to give them the opportunity to move around the organization and learn from multiple perspectives. Let's face it: every missional organization would benefit if the staff serving in programs better understood the marketing and fundraising functions and vice versa.

In the words of Randolph, a global colleague, "There are many women in the ministry already with strong leadership gifts and abilities. As with any professional, some may need intentional development for these leadership gifts and abilities to shine. Let's not assume that the organization's future female leaders are 'out there' somewhere. Many are likely already inside our organization. What is missing is intentional staff development."

• • •

Most importantly, women inside our organizations need prayer. We recently heard of a woman executive joining a missional nonprofit with a spotty history of engaging and keeping their female executive staff. Frankly, the place has been a revolving door for as long as memory holds. We cheered for this woman, high-fived, and then got on our knees. Statistics and the organizational track record are stacked against this new leader. Eight in ten women have not made it in the role she is entering. Why? We believe it is spiritual warfare being waged not just against women but against men and our shared organizational communities. If women were entirely empowered to do the shared work of our organizations, this would have a formidable impact on the powers of poverty and injustice around the world.

TOOLS FOR PEOPLE DEVELOPMENT

Developing people isn't a special event or experience. It's a journey. And for the more challenging development we speak of here—the kind that focuses on creating diversity and cultures of belonging—organizations need new, better tools. The old ways of working and learning together— team building, corporate retreats, seminars, and conferences—won't do the trick here.

Corporate listening sessions. The road toward creating a belonging culture can initially feel downright scary. Gender and race/cultural conversations make people nervous and resistant, and speaking with close colleagues about their personal journey can be threatening. Experienced outside facilitators can be a helpful resource as organizations enter this space. Professional facilitators know how to create safe spaces for discussion on differences. They thrive in making the process enjoyable while still giving opportunities for people to truthfully share their stories and perspectives.

Relationship building. Allowing time and space for people to build relationships beyond their immediate circles can create a huge shift. When spending time together over meals or coffee, participating in small projects, or chatting casually, you get to know someone else's heart. That can go a long way toward moving us to want to advocate for each other, work together, and extend grace for small misunderstandings.

Coaching. A favorite Delaware company has a cultural norm: "Everybody is a coach; everybody gets a coach." By creating the standard that everyone *is* a coach and everyone *gets* coached, we weed out favoritism toward one group of staff over another. Yes, the quality of coaching will vary among individuals, but it is something that can be developed and improved. Most organizations don't provide their leaders with adequate supervisor and coach training. We reward technical expertise with a leadership role and then scratch our heads when it doesn't go well. Every supervisor should be equipped with the basic coaching skills of listening, giving quality feedback, and receiving feedback in a way that doesn't involve an ego-driven or defensive response.

Learning groups and retreats. People are developed best on the job, in the process of everyday work. But there is still a benefit to the occasional retreat away from the day-to-day that allows people a chance to reflect on the organization together, to reflect on their relationships in community with others, and to get restorative time together with colleagues. It is hard for deep conversation to happen in large groups, and smaller learning groups made up of different genders, cultures, and technical skills can help build bridges across the organization. If organizations deployed these diverse learning groups for all kinds of organizational training, the experience could be more enjoyable, meaningful, and memorable.

Measuring and rewarding progress. Part of the process of developing people includes creating metrics for assessing employees around the qualities of the culture organizations are looking for. This requires regularly measuring against progress and celebrating when progress is made. What we celebrate speaks volumes about our organizational culture and what gets passed on to new generations of employees. As the popular business adage goes, "What gets measured—and celebrated—is what matters."

STAYING THE COURSE TO LET IT BEAR FRUIT

Developing people is one of the most difficult functions of an organization. Not because it's technically hard, but because of what it involves. First, developing people means rewiring people's current posture and way of showing up. It includes changing deeply held beliefs about what performance and leadership involve and who gets to have influence. Sometimes it means trying to change long-entrenched behaviors that have never been questioned or challenged before.

Everyone assumes they are an expert in what the culture of the organization should be. From deciding on the core qualities to be developed in employees to determining the best methods of development, *everybody* is an expert. This disagreement can lead to a premature shutdown of too many good leadership programs and processes. If they had only continued long enough, it might have borne fruit in the organization. But this change doesn't happen overnight. It's a journey and it takes time.

It is rare to find leaders with the kind of courage and conviction that sticks around for the long haul. I (Beth) had the opportunity to partner for ten years with one of the biggest missional organizations in the world. They were serious about leadership development and culture change. Together we created and delivered a significant program to develop and diversify the future leadership of the organization. Despite regular budget battles and other executives wanting the headcount attributed to the program, these leaders were committed to both spiritual formation and the development of women. Ninety percent of the participants were from the Global South. Fifty-two percent of the participants were women. At the midpoint of the partnership, our internal tracking showed that 75 percent of the participants had experienced promotions or job expansions, and nearly *all* participants felt a greater sense of loyalty to the organization that had poured into them in such a significant way. The leadership conviction to stay the course got an opportunity to see significant fruit.

A few years later I was involved in creating and executing a program that addressed the need to create a belonging culture at another large organization.

The leadership was on board every step of the way, giving input regularly, growing excited, and speaking of how the program was "just what we need." The CEO and senior leaders participated and shared their own stories of transformation that resulted from their participation in the initial pilot groups. The majority of the participants strongly recommended the program in feedback surveys. However, the program ended abruptly after only six months, at the first sign of pushback from individuals with strong opinions about leadership and the need for hard skills. They saw less importance on the leadership behaviors deemed as "soft skills." They believed that spiritual formation in leadership wasn't necessary. So instead, the organization opted for an off-the-shelf business training that did not acknowledge the organizational priority of belonging. Not surprisingly, the organization didn't stay the course with the second initiative either. Several years have passed and the organization struggles with the same pain points, including inability to hold on to talented female executives.

What was the difference between the two organizations? The leaders of the long-standing program stayed the course. They understood that developing people and cultures takes time, and they were rewarded with a significant return on investment and prestigious standing in the sector today for their diversity and leadership investments. The other organization did not stay the course and are exactly where they started.

Creating cultures of belonging starts with developing *all* our people to move together in the same direction. Workloads, the pace by which we do our work, and the status quo of how we operate today get in the way of change. Developing specific qualities into all our staff and leaders will bring about the new culture we seek.

● ● ●

One more word about empowering women. When we train leaders on empowering women, we always get a comment about the disempowerment of men. Recently an African colleague commented, "I'm seeing all these women rising in the communities in my country. They are being educated and they are receiving important roles in organizations and the government.

This is leaving the men without a role. They used to be the breadwinners; now they are sitting on the stoop without meaning."

Perhaps we hold a similar image of where men will end up if women rise in organizations. A great model of how we can tackle this challenge is Tearfund UK's Transforming Masculinities curriculum. It aims to address this idea in the communities it serves around the world by focusing on creating safer homes and communities by empowering not just women and girls, but men and boys as well. It is not enough for women to feel empowered; men must join in the process. We need this same concept to be brought "in house" in our missional organizations. We need training on how our views on women and men, and the "expected roles" we expect them to perform, have shaped our model of leadership. While we are empowering women, we must empower men to welcome women as co-leaders. And we must empower men to embrace new roles for themselves.

● ● ●

Belonging organizations who are invested in training leaders

- implement educational efforts for *all staff* who invest in core skills such as empathy, listening, and unconscious bias awareness,
- identify and invest in high-potential staff, both women and men, across the organization,
- and intentionally develop and invest in women to become future leaders of the organization.

CHAPTER EIGHT

THE LEADERSHIP WILL TO MAKE A CHANGE

In the last chapter we told a story about two organizations. One succeeded in making a significant investment in their future leaders; the other didn't. The difference wasn't a better program or a more opportune time for implementing leadership training; the difference was leadership will. Many organizational executives plan to train their leaders or invest in diversity "one day," when urgencies and emergencies don't continually hijack the agenda. For most organizations that day never arrives.

We tend to operate in an emergency-response mindset where priorities are triaged to determine what is most pressing and what can be sidelined. When tasked with addressing a tsunami in Asia versus continuing investments in DEI efforts within our organization, market, donor, and staff pressures will always revert to prioritizing the former. But this should not be treated as a zero-sum game. If we continually make that mistake, we prevent ourselves from

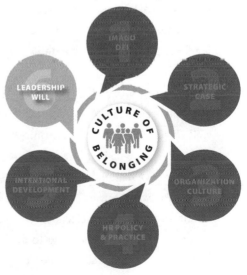

recognizing how much better our organizational response would be if we made the investment in having bold, new, insightful voices around the leadership table. When we continue the good work around the world while building a culture of belonging, our response will be stronger and more creative.

Major pushes toward diversity often have their nexus in organizational crisis or scandal. Like when several senior women or minority staff leave in a short period of time. Or our collective newsfeed is filled with a racial injustice so glaring we cannot ignore it. Or a sexual scandal is exposed in the organization. The response is reactive versus strategic. To avoid a public relations issue, leaders are quick to offer up gender empowerment steps and statements that assure audiences that the problem "will never happen again." Unless we have the will and courage to deal with root causes, it will very likely happen again in some form or another.

What if organizations spent as much time addressing culture as drafting statements?

Most missional organizations are led by good people, doing good work for the world, no doubt. Still, if our sector maintains that we have nothing left to learn about how we can grow beyond current realities, we miss out on how our organizations can become clearer expressions of the kingdom model of leadership and community. Stepping into the arena for the sake of those who have not been included takes boldness and will.

Leadership will—often also called "political will"—is manifested when leaders buy into and articulate a compelling vision, embed it in real accountability for delivery, and begin to expect it throughout the organization. Lack of leadership will, on the other hand, has the same impact on equality efforts as misinterpretations of theology. If not addressed, many if not most of our well-intended efforts will continue to knock against invisible boundaries.

Leaders who live out the will to create more equality demonstrate "strong, visible, active leadership that promotes gender equality tied to strategic organizational outcomes." This kind of leadership is motivated by many different origins. Millennial leaders often demand diversity more naturally than older generations. According to a study, millennials are 25 percent more likely to focus on equality in the workplace than older generations. In chapter four we spoke about how millennials have expectations of greater gender diversity in the workplace because this is what they have gotten accustomed to in the home or at school growing up.

Being a "girl dad" also impacts leadership will. Research shows that fathers of daughters, especially daughters who are the first child, "tend to become less supportive of traditional gender roles and more supportive of anti-discrimination laws, equal pay policies, and sexual harassment enforcement." For others, it is the research case around better business outcomes, innovation, and decision-making that compels a shift in prioritizing diversity.

To other leaders the change comes through relearning theology and understanding how much of the gender roles and norms we societally hold as "absolute truth" are a result of a patriarchal Roman and Greek worldview, as well as scriptural misinterpretation that stands in opposition to the equality and siblinghood Jesus himself came to establish among women and men.

For Craig, the will to make a difference came through a lifetime of learning about the objectives of missional organizations. "Are we fighting poverty, or are we fighting injustice?" he asks. "If leaders feel their work is ending injustice, they *should* see the incongruence between saying, 'We're about empowering women in the communities we serve but we don't care about empowering the women who do the serving.'" While it's easier and faster to deal with the effects rather than the root causes of poverty, organizations must do both: address the effects of poverty *and* the systems that keep people in poverty.

"It's not enough that men use their power for the good of others. What is required is for them to come to the realization that they got their power through unjust systems and need to work to fix those systems," states Prabu, a leader at a major international NGO. For organizations to experience deep, sustained change, the leaders who hold the power must use that power to tear down unjust systems and organizational cultures and recreate new ones where power is shared and where the women in our organizations participate in that shared power.

If we say we believe that empowering women in the communities we serve is the key to better development outcomes, do we believe the same about the women inside our organizations? If we say we stand for increasing agency among our clients, do those who serve in our organizations have the opportunity to experience increased agency in their work? If we ask for men where we serve to include women in decision making that impacts the entire community—whether in agriculture, health, or infrastructure—do we ask the men in our organizations to do the same?

"Our commitment is to diversity in the recruitment of the next CEO," read one statement on social media announcing the retirement of a tenured sector leader. We have seen a number of these types of exits into retirement, where senior leaders finally find the courage and desire to advocate for greater diversity as they head out the door. This is valuable and reflects the journey many leaders are on during their lifetime. The challenge we speak of here is to stand for diversity even when it comes at a cost to our own leadership expansion *now*.

Courageous leaders are willing to confront their own personal fears about change and what it may cost them and push forward anyway. Whether they are convinced by good business strategy or guided by their personal values, they are able to push through criticisms to do what is right for the organization. Courageous leaders surround themselves with different viewpoints, people who come from different backgrounds, and those with unique lived experiences. They give up their share of power and platform frequently to allow women and colleagues of color to genuinely lead. While choosing to lead this way may result in longer time spent developing ideas and strategy, what gets developed is more likely to be successful *and* owned by more people in the organization, making it more sustainable.

PRIVILEGE

After one organization launched a diversity initiative, we started seeing reviews pop up on the Glassdoor workplace review site. They stated, "Women have equal opportunity; they shouldn't expect equal representation," and,

> White Males Need Not Apply: If you are a white male, don't bother coming here. You're not wanted. And if you are a white male that already works here, don't expect a promotion anytime soon. Apparently, it's our fault that the organization has maintained a masculine norm in leadership positions in the past, so the rest of us will have to pay the

price to show how "diverse" we are. The organization has gone too far and will not promote or hire any more white males into leadership positions. It's outright discrimination to appease the women who have been crying foul. Not saying they're wrong. But discriminating against white males to make the women happy is wrong.

Dr. Christena Cleveland is a researcher of privilege. "When privileged people are required to participate in a system of equality where everyone gets the same resources and they don't get any extra boost, it feels like discrimination to them," she states. "The psychological experience is comparable to the experience that women of color experience when they are *actually* being discriminated against." Those who have benefited from long-standing norms, such as those male employees who posted on Glassdoor, feel like they are being discriminated against just because the organization is making efforts to elevate women and minoritized colleagues in the leadership.

They are oblivious to the discrimination women face in their work. Sure, in theory women and colleagues of color have equal opportunities for leadership, but in reality, they receive far less intentional investment for senior roles, fewer opportunities for growth, and more experiences of being passed over when leadership roles are awarded. The statistics don't lie. Bias exists in all areas of organizational culture, from hiring to investing to promoting, as White male–dominated leadership teams unconsciously attract and promote people who continue to provide a familiar leadership model. Missional organizations can prepare for pushback in the form of these anonymous Glassdoor commenters. But they must acknowledge that shouts of "foul" don't represent discrimination but a correction of decades of wrong made right can help stay the course to equality.

Another form of pushback is the fear of conservative donors and audiences thinking, "We are becoming a feminist organization?" Pro-women and pro-equality agendas can be labeled as "feminist," and there are many who are threatened by the term.

Missional organizations have engaged in deep learning conversations with conservative donors and churches about the calling of Christians to advocate for welcoming the stranger or helping people living with HIV. These were both initially considered controversial topics among conservative audiences. The invitation is to engage in similar conversations around welcoming women and minoritized leaders into equal standing. These conversations with broad audiences are an opportunity to share learning about the positive impact and influence missional organizations will experience as a result.

Women also need to examine their own courage in making change. Executives often lament the lack of internal female candidates who apply for leadership roles. There are many reasons for this, but if we want to see change happen in our organizations, women must press into their fear and put themselves in the candidate pool for leadership.

Women and other minoritized staff also need courage to bring to light an unwelcoming culture. Shelly shares an example with us: "My organization organized a women's leadership lunch with female executives and board members in attendance. I don't think the male executives realized that women don't meet without the topic of workplace inequality coming up. It always comes up because it's an experience shared by all women. As I was the most senior woman there, my bosses thought I had organized some kind of a revolt and were concerned because there were board members present. The next Monday I got called in by HR for a 'talking to' and a few months later I was offered a sizable severance package. That's how afraid the organization was of women speaking of these issues together." Women may experience pushback for speaking up in the form of marginalization, being overlooked for advancement, or even exited from the organization.

Senior leaders won't often own up to these actions. No, it is done more subtly. There will be excuses like, "She wasn't a good fit," or, "We needed to go a different direction." The same organizations may praise a vocal male executive for his "welcome disruption," or say, "We need more straight talk like this in our organization," but similar strength and directness are rarely accepted from women.

BEING AN ALLY

If you are a male colleague or leader reading this book, you are a wonderful ally already just for thinking deeply about what is missing in our sector. But our best intentions need to be reexamined. How can we say, "I empower you,"

"I will hold the microphone for you," "I will be the shoulders you can stand on," and "I will give up my seat for you," when at the end of the day we still have the power to disempower others? What will keep us from pulling back the microphone when we don't like what is being said or shrugging our shoulders away when the weight becomes heavy?

In the diversity space, discussions are focusing on the concept of being a champion—a leader who advocates for women and minorities in their leadership role, an ally, any man who is willing to take up the cause of gender or racial justice to create a belonging environment for everyone.

But rarely do real allies need titles.

Prabu speaks to us about being an ally. "As a young man, I saw my father hit my mother," he says. "So I was resolved that I would never beat a woman. I never felt that it made me a good person; it was just me saying, 'I don't want to be like that.'"

As a teen, Prabu found himself being verbally abusive and controlling toward a girlfriend. "I didn't make the connection between that behavior and my father's. I felt like my behavior was normal since there was no resistance and nobody told me it was wrong. In my culture everyone was doing it. It wasn't until I heard a message at church about doing *more* with my life that the scales started to fall away, and I began to see things differently.

"I realized I was no better than my father," Prabu continues. "I think that's why I am so uncomfortable with putting men on pedestals as allies. Because we're all on a spectrum. There are no good or bad guys; we each live within that spectrum."

Later in his career working on projects that supported women, Prabu had an aha moment:

> I realized that men need to be part of this conversation, because most often we are the ones benefiting from the way things are, and we are the ones doing the abusing. For a long time, I struggled with campaigns that focused on fatherhood and caregiving behaviors, for example, because they didn't talk about seeing the woman as an equal. These programs focused only on external behaviors but didn't try to change the value men place on women or unpack gender norms and what it means to be a man or what it means to be a woman. If men

continue to believe they are superior to women, then the more extreme behaviors like beating will continue.

As long as we're not challenging an unequal system in our community and in our own thinking, all of the rest of our interventions will be at surface level. The danger of this is that we applaud the changed surface-level behaviors, but we don't tackle the cultures and issues that result in the abuse and devaluing of women in the first place. I've also seen that when men receive pushback from other men in the community, they revert back to the behaviors they once had and there is no deep-rooted transformation. There is no conviction of a new way of being because it's the *right thing* to do.

When we left the conversation with Prabu, we reflected on his words, replacing "my culture" with "the organizational culture." It highlighted the enormity of the challenge we are facing in creating cultural change. Courageous leaders are needed now more than ever. Prabu's story shows that becoming an ally to women is a journey. It's not an immediate decision; it's a series of experiences that continue to sharpen and refine our thinking and commitment to the work we are called to.

On this journey male allies can do simple things to support women every day. Here are some suggestions for staying the course of being an ally:

Model the way. Establish a culture that balances work and personal life commitments by being a good leader *and* an engaged parent, spouse, friend. Ask people when they are taking vacation and let others know when you will be taking yours. Share stories with your team about the care work you share with your partner. Let people in on the burden of leadership you personally experience.

Challenge marginalization. In meetings, is there a trend of marginalization? Are women always the ones tasked with getting coffee or taking notes? Offer to do some of that yourself or delegate it to someone else in the meeting. Set up a rotation for taking notes, preparing for the next meeting, and ordering the catering.

Listen better. If this is not something you have cultivated, practice by putting aside distractions when you are meeting with people. Leave your phone, your computer, and your notepaper behind when you're meeting a colleague for coffee or lunch. Position yourself with the fewest distractions possible so you can be fully present.

Help others listen better too. In meetings, do women rarely speak up? Are they spoken over when they do contribute? Be intentional to insert something like this into the conversation: "I think Beth was just cut off and I'd like to hear the rest of her point."

Give credit. Pay attention when you notice women's ideas being hijacked midmeeting, and redirect the credit for comment back to the woman who said it: "That's a great point, and I think that's what Eeva was just saying. Eeva, can you elaborate?"

Challenge groupthink. When unfair "groupthink" is downplaying a woman's contribution, speak up rather than going along with the group. Say something like, "Wow, I'm surprised by your assessment. My experience in working with Amy is totally different based on the project she led really skillfully." Ask for specifics when someone makes a vague complaint about a colleague.

Be an advocate. In rooms where there are no women, ask, "Where are the women? Are we missing a voice here?" Also make it a point to advocate for the women you know who would be great for the promotion, project, or stretch assignment. Be willing to speak up and have that hard conversation when you hear men make sexist comments or allude to any form of sexism, sexual harassment, or other misconduct.

Build your own healthy team culture. Don't wait for someone else to model the way—you be the role model. Create a healthy culture by ensuring that team-building activities are held during work hours, allowing all members to participate. Welcome diverse input into critical ideas and strategy, ensuring meetings allow everyone to use their voice. Model receiving opinions and inputs that others may deem as "critical." Share the stage, the microphone, and the accolades when teams accomplish good things. Don't do it so people will think of you as a "good guy"; do it because it's right.

Be an activist for positive change. Cause some "good trouble," as Congressman John Lewis would say. We are tired of leaders sitting in the room where it happens but *not* leading, *not* causing anyone to think or behave differently. Leadership takes courage, requires risk, and calls you to do the right thing.

CHALLENGING BOARDS TO GET ON BOARD

Creating and fostering a new culture doesn't happen overnight. It requires leadership will and accountability at all levels and for the long haul. A board of directors has the responsibility and singular ability to influence organizational strategy and senior executive behavior. As busy professionals and experts in their own fields, board members join the organization out of deep love for the cause. They have the ability to affect not only organizational strategy but cultural strategy. They can expect that management will pursue healthy cultures, where people feel a sense of belonging, by holding the CEO responsible.

The challenge is that organizations are governed by mostly White male board members. Lack of board diversity is a problem across all sectors in the United States, with too few women and too few people of color chairing and serving on boards. This happens mostly by the way in which board members are recruited. Both the current board and the CEO recruit new board members, and "like hires like" unless diverse candidates are intentionally sought. Many donors, foundations, and nonprofit monitoring agencies like Charity Navigator are starting to track and reward diversity among boards, CEOs, and executive teams. The hope is that this pressure creates needed change.

If missional organizations start showing up at the bottom of the list of "best places to work for women" and understand the coming talent wars as the millennial generation becomes the majority of the workforce in 2025, we expect the sector to pursue in response to this as well.

A strategy that prioritizes creating a culture of belonging can make a genuine impact. The board has a key role in creating this strategy. But board members are rarely from the missional sector and rather consist of high-achieving leaders who may lack understanding about the context in which missional organizations work, including what best practices look like in the operations and programs they perform. This may mean misunderstanding the strategy of the very organization they are committed to overseeing.

As an example, one of the most important functions of the board is to hire the CEO. If the board is not well aware of the history of gender disparity across the sector, organizations will continue to be led by people we are accustomed to seeing, despite the myriad of qualified female leaders available for every CEO seat in the sector. In a recent search, a board chair explained to the leadership team, "Yes, we wanted a new style of leadership; yes, we wanted diversity; but in the end we decided to go with the man who had CEO experience." This chairman was unaware of the realities of the missional sector, where very few women and people of color have made it to the CEO role and gained the CEO experience he was looking for. Creating a new leadership strategy for an organization requires that the board is aware of the obstacles that exist. Boards hold the tools to break the glass ceilings that remain in place in nearly all missional organizations. This is the kind of courage boards should be tasked with.

Here are the actions every board should take toward creating a culture of belonging:

Hire a female CEO. Or at least become educated about the biases you may individually or collectively hold and consider training to fix that. Recently a major nonprofit selected a diverse CEO selection committee and required that the committee participate in diversity training before even one candidate stepped in front of them.

Ask to see the strategic plan. If it doesn't involve creating a culture that centers belonging and monitors progress on a routine basis through agreed-upon metrics, or if the organization is not making progress in such a plan, ask why.

Require a line item in the annual budget. This budget line should support DEI efforts in the organization, whether in salary of dedicated staff, training investments, or annual events that center diversity. This is not a "one and done" effort but rather requires ongoing cultivation and intentionality. A board chair of a large NGO once said, "The budget is the key strategic document of our organization. On these lines you will see what matters to us the most." How can an organization claim to care about diversity if it's not included in the budget?

Review key metrics. Organizations "measure what matters." Establish and regularly review key indicators such as employee and leader demographic breakdown, pay equity, hiring and promotion practices, and others.

Read reviews by past employees. These can be internal to the organization or on a website like Glassdoor. Monitoring staff satisfaction is usually past the purview of the board, but if diversity is a central value to the organization, board members and management should have conversations about employee feedback regarding efforts and success.

Request survey results. Find out if employee feedback surveys include questions specific to a culture of belonging, such as:

- "I see strong executive leadership support of my organization's value of diversity and inclusion."
- "People of all cultures and backgrounds are respected and valued here."
- "I feel included and respected in this organization."
- "I am comfortable talking about my background and cultural experiences with my colleagues."

Invest in training. Participate in board workshops on bias training and diversity. If these are not routinely offered for the board, advocate for them.

Set key goals. Tie CEO performance reviews and annual pay raises to successful achievement of key diversity indicators and goals. What gets measured gets done.

Most nonprofit employees don't understand the board's limited role and are often discouraged when the board does nothing to save them from inept, blatantly bad, or even corrupt leadership at the top of the organization. The good news is that strong nonprofit boards exercise their governance beyond a narrow fiduciary role to ensure an ethic of care toward employees of the organization. While this is rare, it is emerging as an industry best practice.

A CALL FOR FOUNDATIONS AND DONORS TO EXPECT MORE

One of the fastest ways for the missional sector to become cultures of belonging is for foundations, donors, and watchdog groups to change the way they evaluate and fund organizations. Metrics of success needs to expand to include not only how many houses we have built but how we have created a culture where the very best of our talent is being built and promoted toward the work we're investing in.

Nonprofit organizations could be experiencing 25 to 35 percent greater impact if they ensured greater diversity on their leadership teams. Despite the significant research around this reality, foundations and individual donors rarely ask questions about diversity in leadership when making their funding decisions. When funding organizations fail to measure how well an organization is doing internally, there is no impetus to change.

Here are actions that donors and watchdog agencies could take to improve nonprofit performance:

Review the leadership and board diversity of the organization. Ensure the organization isn't "hiding" its lack of diversity by putting all levels of leadership on its executive webpage. Look for titles like SVP, VP, or C-suite roles to determine the executive makeup of the organization. One research team started the interesting process of reviewing organizational 990 forms and comparing this to "leadership" webpages. They told an entirely different story about who the senior leaders are.

Require reporting. Ask to see statistics on executive team and board diversity, leadership at each level of the organization, and pay equity, as well as the organizational diversity statement or policy. Better yet, tie this data to approval of new funding.

THE LESSONS WE'VE FORGOTTEN—WHAT DOES IT MEAN TO DIE TO SELF?

"The problem of toxic masculinity *is* the problem of toxic masculinity. It's so ingrained in the people and the culture of the organization that changing it is hard. How do you ask someone to die to self?" asks Craig.

When we were children, most of us were taught by our parents to share our toys, and sharing made the time of play more enjoyable for everyone. But it also meant we had to let go of what was in our hands for someone else to enjoy for a while. As youth, if we were lucky, we had coaches who taught us that it was important for everyone to get playing time in the game. But it also meant we had to sit on the bench while others on the team got the chance to develop their abilities.

Somewhere along the way as we moved from childhood and youth to adulthood, when we weren't paying attention, our language became "*my* organization, *my* career, *my* leadership." We lost the ability to see where we might need to sacrifice or take a turn stepping out of leadership in order to make space for others. We have forgotten lessons of our youth.

In a talk about privilege, Dr. Christena Cleveland shares the familiar story of the bleeding woman who touched the hem of Jesus. Jesus, on his way to heal Jairus's daughter, stopped and turned all his attention to her. The crowd surrounding Jesus was also forced to stop and to observe what was happening. Jesus stood and listened to the woman, and, as the book of Mark states, she "told him the whole truth" (Mark 5:33). In her creative way, Cleveland guesses that the woman took her time—perhaps for the first time in her life all attention was suddenly on her. Jairus, a ruler in the synagogue, probably wanted to rush her along. It would have been completely understandable given the urgency of the situation with his dying daughter and his position of influence in the community.

But Jairus didn't do it. Instead he waited patiently, listened, and heard her story. And in the waiting and the listening, Jairus died to his own agenda and urgency in the moment. He died to self.

This is the cost of making room for others: to hear their stories, to enter into their experiences, and to find common belonging there.

While they were all waiting, Jairus learned that his daughter had died. The thing he feared most and the reason he had come to Jesus for help had happened.

What does it mean to die to self? It means seeing other people. Really seeing. It means leaders exercising their leadership will and sacrificing their agenda for the sake of others on the margins, releasing them to stand in the center. It means believing in the God of abundance, not scarcity. When we do so, God reveals his abundance and meets our needs as well.

In the story of Jairus, Jesus ends up resurrecting Jarius's daughter.

Belonging organizations that demonstrate leadership will for greater inclusion . . .

- realize the role current leaders play in modeling the courage and will needed to make an organizational change,

- perform a regular assessment of organizational climate to determine how female leaders and staff members view their role and influence in the organization,

- and display leadership behaviors that give preference to those excluded from leadership tables, even if it means dying to their own agendas and privilege.

CHAPTER NINE

WOMEN AND MEN BEYOND
THE WORKPLACE

One woman shares in an op-ed, "How much longer could I keep this juggling act up? Not much longer. I felt stretched, overwhelmed, and at times as if my best efforts to keep it all together weren't good enough. Like many women across the country, I have internalized the burden of care. As a working woman who decided to have children, I believed it was my job to figure it all out."

These are the words of a working mother describing the impact of the Covid-19 pandemic on her daily life.

We wrote this book in the middle of the pandemic, starting in the months leading up to 2020 and finishing at a time when the future still seems obscure. Writing during these months hasn't been easy—a sentiment echoed in our conversations with other leaders, advocates, and writers, no matter what topic each was grappling with. The question on everyone's lips was: What will the world look like when this is all over? And will what we are saying still be relevant in the "new normal"?

But for women, the new normal is the old normal.

Women exited the workforce at staggering numbers during the pandemic. Nearly 3 million women in the United States have dropped out of the workforce, and women's employment fell by 4.2 percent globally, with 54 million women (and counting) losing their jobs. The pandemic and its far-reaching impact further exposed the fragile roles women still play in families, societies, and workplaces; some in the media accurately called it "women's preexisting condition." Social distancing, intended to protect people from harm, put women in danger of increased domestic violence in their own homes. Women's fragile employment in care and service industries was the most dispensable. Female-dominated sectors like education, hospitality, and food industries took the hardest hit. And women were the ones picking up the extra labor in the home and their communities, many at the cost of their careers.

These compounding struggles have revealed a plain truth for all to see: women are often left alone to figure it all out.

Spaces outside the workplace offer men and women opportunities to collaborate to create a fairer and more sustainable division of labor. These feed into the ways women will succeed inside organizations. Women and men together have an invitation to reinvestigate and question the roles they are expected to perform in societies, organizations, and homes. Without a doubt this happens at an individual level, inside private homes, and between partners, and this is a welcome conversation and a shift from decades past. But this conversation—about what is fair—must happen inside missional organizations too.

Men who are allies to women inside their organization can fearlessly question their own attitudes and biases. They can create change with small but meaningful actions.

UNPAID WORK

"Other countries have social safety nets. The US has women," states sociologist Jessica Calarco. "Women in the US have long done a disproportionate share of the unpaid service work in institutions and at home." According to a recent study, the monetary value of women's global unpaid care work is at least $10.9 trillion annually. This is a massive number in proportion to the $88 trillion global economy, representing the largest individual—and unaccounted for—"industry." In the United States, where the total economy equals $21.4 trillion, unpaid labor of women totals $1.5 trillion. The number is enormous.

Leaving unpaid work out of GDP calculations was a conscious choice in the 1950s. In her book *Invisible Women,* author Caroline Criado Perez writes, "Everyone acknowledges that there is economic value in that work, it's just not part of the economy." She asserts that this work was omitted from calculations not because it was deemed irrelevant but because "it would be too big a task in terms of collecting data."

Every country, community, church, organization, and family benefits from women's unpaid labor. And even though free work by women is not included in calculations of the global economy, that does not mean it is unimportant—it is the backbone of the economy. From a purely economic standpoint it's easy to see why there is such a low incentive to figure out infrastructures and policies that acknowledge and start paying for unpaid labor. If the worst that can happen is a million-woman march on Washington once a decade or "angry feminists" railing mostly in echo chambers, it's a risk communities and organizations are willing to take. They count on the reality that at the end of the day women are going to continue to do what needs to get done for their families and communities.

Continuing to hold on to a worldview that limits women's roles provides a simple solution to an economic problem. No matter how favorably we personally think of gender equality in theory, in practice, few are willing to pay the cost of true equality. We have been socialized with the notion that free work is "women's work," but we rarely question the enormous economic, cultural, political, and even religious powers that have led us to assume that this is true.

Even those of us who are furthest along on our journey toward equality rarely question the idea that childcare, eldercare, education, cleaning, grooming, shopping, and food preparation are tasks reserved for women. These tasks show up at workplaces, too, in the shape of ordering lunches, taking notes, maintaining diversity or other affinity groups, and organizing meetings and special events. Men participate in these tasks also, but studies show that men's free labor consists of half the hours that women's do, and the accolades men receive for picking up the coffee cups after a meeting or "babysitting" their own kids speak to the culturally shared understanding that they are just helping women with *their* work.

The economic argument also supports the persisting gender wage gap where women overall earn 82 cents to a White man's dollar for the same job. Of this, Black women earn 63 cents and Latinas 55 cents to a White man's dollar. Because women's employment is seen as temporary and an exception, women's participation is also considered less valuable. There is an economic argument that life events impacting women, namely childbirth, are deemed either a benefit or a selective "opt-out" of the workforce that come at a cost to the organization, and women should be penalized for the indulgence by lower wages.

Many organizations also hold on to the "living wage" mindset, where men earn the main income in a household and should be thus paid more for equal work. Lea, an HR professional, admits that before becoming aware of gender bias impacting wages, she would often consider requests for raises based on people's family situations: "If I knew that a man was the main breadwinner in their home, I took their request for a raise more seriously than a single woman's, even if they held the same title and had the same amount of responsibility."

There remains a cemented economic interest in making sure women's primary role and *most important* work is free and unpaid. As a result, despite women representing 40 percent of the global workforce, and 50 percent in the United States, women's employment continues to be considered an exception to male employment.

Every woman's salary that is lower for equal work, every time a woman is not heard in a meeting, every time women do not participate in the design of shared work and schedules, the same bottom-line message is communicated: "Your real work is at home." Even though women now equal men in the workplace, their employment is still seen as temporary and dispensable. And this impacts *all* women, whether they are mothers or plan to ever become mothers or not.

This reality reflects an invitation to missional organizations that are serious about equal treatment of women.

One organization decided to run the data on women and men inside their structures. They discovered that most women who entered junior roles in the organization exited five to seven years later, at around the time they had a child.

The data showed that the majority of senior women, those who could afford it, stayed on after the birth of a baby. The organization was churning through cohort after cohort of junior women without a plan on how to keep them as their life circumstances changed. In practice this may have seemed like the more affordable option, but in reality, the cost of losing all that technical and organizational expertise and recruiting and training new staff was high.

When missional organizations become serious about fair wages for women, they have many tools at their disposal.

Managers can take inventory of the types of free labor women perform inside the organization beyond their written job description. While these activities are legitimate in the "other tasks as assigned" category, for many women they can add up to several hours of additional work every week. Inventory can help us find out if women are disproportionately organizing meals and events, facilitating extracurricular staff activities, or taking notes and creating agendas. In a workplace invested in parity, women and men can begin to share in this work evenly. Or these tasks can be added to someone's job description and reasonably compensated for.

Organizations can also run data on wage gaps for women. Are there certain job categories that are majority women, especially in the lower-paid "care" category? Are women and men receiving equal pay for equal work or could the "head of household" mindset be at play? Are women's titles and salaries rightsized for equal work? Publicizing salary ranges and creating a plan on how to catch up staff whose salaries are lagging also creates confidence around fairness among employees.

Percy spoke to us about a team member who took maternity leave leading up to performance evaluation season. She questioned whether this employee should receive a full cost-of-living increase or only a partial one since she didn't have a full twelve months of performance data to review her on. "When I discussed the situation with HR," explains Percy, "I realized that I absolutely needed to give her the increase. Sky-high inflation had impacted every member of the team no matter what their life situation. And I did not want to penalize my team member for having a baby; I wanted to relate to it as a normal life event our organization makes room for in our budgets and practices."

MICROECONOMIES

Because I (Eeva) grew up surrounded by women who not only worked but pursued meaningful careers, it never occurred to me not to work. And as first-generation immigrants—my husband and I came with two suitcases—we both *had to* work. I didn't grow up with an expectation that my husband would be the provider and I would be the caregiver; I assumed we would share those roles, and blessedly so did my husband.

The cultural worldview that states that a "woman's place is in the home" has formed how society thinks of women's time and availability. As a new mom I realized quickly that expectations on women have been built around the idea of my constant availability. Churches organize women's Bible studies in the middle of the workday. Preschools end their programs in the middle of the day. Schools assume women's ability to volunteer as a classroom parent, in the PTA, or with bake sales and lunches. School days that let out early or hold afternoon baseball games assume that a parent is available to be there, and the families who are not able to be there all the time experience enormous social pressure and guilt.

And workplace cultures don't routinely account for these pressures. Rather they can make it difficult or culturally unacceptable for employees to leave in the middle of a workday to tend to a sick child or to ask for an afternoon off for a game or recital, and parents are left in constant negotiation about whose work and schedule is more important and less flexible. Mothers and fathers are required to toggle between work and everything else and end up getting burned out by it. Sheryl Sandberg famously describes in her book *Lean In* how she would tiptoe out of the office at 5:30 p.m. so she could nurse her newborn son before bedtime but also so she wouldn't communicate lack of commitment to her job.

As a young mom, I too tried to set up my schedule in ways that ensured my maximum availability in all aspects of life: parenting, work, volunteering at church, and even as a partner to my husband. For several years I kept this up, mindlessly running from task to task, going through the motions of what I thought being a good mother, employee, and partner looked like. I was exhausted. At the same time, I was reading and learning about gender equality. By the time my kids were nearing middle school and they began to show signs of independence, I came to an important realization: this whole thing—expectations of availability, perfection, and constant care—is "human made."

And if it's made by humans, humans—like me—can undo it.

Embracing essentialism. A friend decided to quit a big leadership role with a missional organization and stay home with her newborn son. "I just hate the idea of being less than perfect in everything I'm doing," she explained. In her situation, she could easily afford the decision: her husband earned a huge paycheck. But what about everyone else? What about single mothers or households that rely on two incomes? What about couples where the husband is sick and cannot work?

The rest of us must be okay with less than perfect.

Marcia, a friend working a high-level leadership role, has made up a "70 percent rule" for herself. She loves how upset it makes her (kid-free) male colleagues when she states, "My expectation of myself is to show up at 70 percent of everything I do." Unheard of! An employee who doesn't show up at 110 percent? Marcia realized that if she was going to do all the things on her list, she had to lower the bar for herself and the expectations of those around her. She began by asking herself, as she reviewed her calendar each day, what could she skip? What could she delegate? What could she do her best on and hand off to others to review and improve? She states, "The saying 'always be the hardest worker in the room' for me became, 'know what is yours to do in the room and focus on that.'"

In his book *Essentialism,* Gregg McKeown states, "It is not about how to get more things done; it's about how to get the right things done. It doesn't mean just doing less for the sake of less either. It is about making the wisest possible investment of your time and energy in order to operate at our highest point of contribution by doing only what is essential."

This idea has resonated with Marcia. "Thinking of every area in my life through this lens of essentialism became lifesaving for me, but it also meant 'training' those around me," she says.

For many families this means shaking up expectations of being a perfect wife and mother (whatever that is). Roles and responsibilities for families can become something they agree to *inside* the family: if it works for them, it works. Examples might include skipping draining activities such as unnecessary school shopping, putting on massive birthday parties, and preparing elaborate school lunches. Instead, families can focus on things they truly all enjoy: good family dinners (prepared by mom *or* dad or the restaurant down the street) or fifteen-minute conversations about our day instead of feeling bad about hours spent apart.

Women and men must dare to question the messages they receive every day about what good performance—whether in motherhood, fatherhood, or employment—looks like. Who set the bar? Who created the expectations? And were those expectations created to serve a particular economic or cultural agenda? Questioning expectations and setting our own rules for home and work requires courage.

At work essentialism means agreement with the boss on how performance is measured. You can't hit a bull's-eye if you don't know what the target is, and the target for work should be very precisely defined. One boss routinely stated to his team, "I like when employees surprise me with their performance." Bull's-eye performance is the opposite of that: no surprises are required. Every week and every day, we know exactly what we need to do to perform on the "good to excellent" end of the scale, and this has nothing to do with perfection—it has to do with solid, routine performance. In practice this results in weekly conversations between managers and team members about goals and priorities.

For organizations this means using an individualized approach with employees in establishing how they meet performance goals. It becomes less about the nine-to-five and more about the exact work each employee does on a team. Georgia, an administrator in a nonprofit, tells us, "During Covid I was straddling my kids' school and my work—they had to happen at the same time. I thought I was doing my best until my boss emailed me and said, 'I noticed you are stacking your emails. I'd like to see them come in throughout the day so I know you're at your desk.'" This posture is the polar opposite of the type of flexibility many women need. Instead, managers should work with their team members to define expectations and measure those instead.

Rethinking ambition. Christina describes designing a space for herself, as she saw her grandmother do many years prior. "I lived with my grandmother for a couple of years in Chicago after finishing college," says Christina. "Her grit and strong work ethic influenced me. She was the daughter of an immigrant and moved from rural North Dakota to Chicago at fourteen so she could start a career. She was an urban, modern, strong woman who created systems of efficiency at home and worked full-time into her eighties. She kept up on the news, thought for herself, and dressed fashionably until the day she died. She had high expectations and always believed the best was possible."

Christina did karate from an early age at a high level. Karate was a male-dominated sport at the time and growing up in it as a young girl shaped her life. She learned to push the boundaries, break through stereotypes, and challenge the status quo. Becoming an elite athlete also shaped how she views growth and potential. Christina continues,

> But as a young mom, I found myself being frustrated because I felt I had to be perfect, and that perfect meant staying home with my kids. Instead, I had to discover my own path in motherhood. For a while I tried a hybrid of part-time work and part-time stay-at-home parenting. Eventually I realized that was actually harder than working full-time and splitting the home and parenting responsibilities with my husband. I believe that I'm a better mom when I am fully alive as a person pursuing my own passions on top of parenting. It was good for my kids, my marriage, and myself.
>
> I became a CEO early on. I had always wanted to run a company; I just didn't know how I was going to get there. Part of this desire was ambition and wanting to have a meaningful impact, but part of it was also wanting to create a culture that supports working parents. I guess, as a working mother, I created the career that I needed.
>
> I think there's a misconception that, as a woman, charting and planning a course means that we are not waiting on God's will. But I think creating goals and working toward them is actually part of God's desire for us. Live so I can give has become a life principle of mine. It means that I must have something to give something. I must be alive to give life. Women need resources to be able to give their money, or time, or energy.

Jenny grew up in an immigrant community. She told us,

> My parents are first-generation Korean Americans. I grew up in a community of very hardworking people. I was expected to do well, and I guess I was always ambitious. I realized early on that we need women

in leadership of organizations, companies, and movements to make a difference. As an Asian American woman, I am often the only one representing a certain value, and there are still times when I don't speak up in a meeting because I think what I'm saying is not valued. I know I have to speak up, so I give myself a pep talk to believe I belong in the room.

For a woman to have ambition is to carve out her calling in the ways she is gifted and what God has created her for. Becoming a mother hasn't changed my career trajectory, but it has changed how I express my ambition. I am more mindful of my time and my commitments now. I used to travel and work all the time, but that is time I miss spending with my boys. So, these days I'm not working all the time.

I've realized that ambition is also saying "no" to opportunities, Our "no" can help refine our mission in life. For young women I encourage them to be ambitious in ways that affirm who they are naturally and doesn't detract. For women of color, I say, "Say no to giving free advice and strategy that doesn't pay for the years of experience you've accumulated." To women in general I say, "We're raised to be service-oriented but it's okay to say 'no.'"

Ambition is not a dirty word. Women and men need healthy, righteous ambition to achieve the important work of our organizations. Instead, in our organizations we can learn to recognize healthy ambition and how it is manifested in ways that feel natural to women and men in their various life situations.

Missional organizations want to employ people who are ambitious and highly engaged with their work. Studies show that people who are ambitious have higher levels of accomplishment in the domains of education and employment. Success in these domains, in turn, can translate to higher overall satisfaction with life. However, limiting ambition to education and work reveals only a part of what is possible. The women we interviewed, all highly accomplished in their careers, spoke of ambition as mothers, as advocates, and as women of faith. This is what organizations can learn from women's ambition. They can broaden it to include being a partner, parent, friend, and community member. It can mean drawing less from career identity and more from meaningful, deep connections with family, community, and faith. Our careers and job identities are not permanent, and even during our career years, we are called to be, as a one female CEO states it, "more than just one thing." We are all called to a journey of peeling back the layers of identity and belonging from the temporal to the eternal.

Organizations must let women partake in ambition and manifest it in ways that feel natural to them. This means reclaiming ambition for women and men to share and partake of together. We often link ambition to the pursuit of selfish gain and forget that healthy, righteous ambition is needed by women and men to live out in the fullness God has created both to be and to achieve the important work of our organizations.

Executives sometimes wonder about women, "I don't know if she really wants to lead." Sure, if we limit leadership ambition to male behaviors only, we may not recognize when a woman is presenting ambition. Women are extremely ambitious for the success of their team, the well-being of their people, achieving the organization's mission while not allowing work to override the rest of life to the detriment of family, health, and general wholeness. If ambition equals self-promotion, sixty-hour workweeks, and a hunger for winning at any cost—yeah, she may not want that.

Missional organizations that want to celebrate and promote women who manifest their ambition in different ways should broaden conversations about what healthy ambition looks like. If an organization has prioritized a driven leadership model, acceptable forms of ambition might currently include working over Sabbath, expansion over excellence, efficiency over slowing down to allow the last and the least to catch up. If we expand our understanding of ambition, instead of saying, "She likes to take a long vacation each year; I don't think she's serious about her work or leadership material," we can say, "She makes family her priority by taking a long vacation every year. That's the kind of leadership we are looking for in our family-friendly organizational culture." Both women and men can flourish in an organization that believes in that kind of healthy ambition.

Relying on others for help. Amy is lead pastor of a large church in Baltimore. "There is a cultural narrative that women must care about other people more than they care about themselves, and I have faced opposition in my career because of it," she tells us. "It is still breaking a social contract when a woman pursues goals outside the home."

As a young child Amy felt a call to ministry inspired by the sense of community in her childhood church. "In high school, I became interested in how people make meaning of the world and how they relate to God," she says. "I don't think I could be anything else but a minister."

Amy always knew she wanted to have children, but she also wanted to continue her work. She had watched her own mother experience a season of questioning her purpose after her kids were grown. There was a sense of mourning in her mother's life that she didn't want to experience.

Amy says, "I finished my PhD between my two children's fourth birthdays, and it wasn't easy. I spent a lot of Saturdays at the library and worried about missing kids' activities. I knew that it was only for a short amount of time and my husband cared for our kids as well as I did. I knew this was what I was meant to do with my gifts and abilities. Now I realize that it's important for both me and my husband to show our son and daughter an example of how to live out *their* gifts and abilities."

Women rely on support to get through the busy years.

Some women have a trusted partner, like Amy, and others rely on a whole network of partners, grandparents, aunts and uncles, teachers, neighbors, friends, and paid or traded help to make it all work. These important groups of people support and surround each other to make life and work possible. They consist of individuals who share schedules, coordinate care, arrange transportation and meals, and do all the other little things that need to happen in a day. When I (Eeva) was a working mother of two elementary-age kids, my "village" consisted of my husband, mother, sisters, teachers, several trustworthy friends, and even my boss and coworkers.

Organizations and individual managers have many tools at their disposal to help them join an employee's circle of support—their village. This may mean completely rethinking someone's assignment or simply offering small acts of flexibility and outside-the-box thinking about distribution of workloads and schedules. It starts with the acknowledgment of the important responsibilities employees participate in outside of work and sharing in the burden of getting it all done.

This is countercultural, we realize.

The norm has been that people show up to work as their work personas, hiding away the inconvenient parts of themselves like families, other care work, even mental or physical health issues. But a belonging organization welcomes conversations about the support employees need for the "other parts" of their lives.

A THIRD SPACE FOR A POST-COVID ORGANIZATION

Children growing up overseas know what it means to be a "third culture kid." This is the term coined for children of missionaries, diplomats, and military personnel who brought their own first culture to a different country and went on to form a third culture, a sort of consolidation of the two. This space between what is and what could or must be—the third space—is what we create when reality fails us. The third space theory suggests that an "ambiguous" area is born when two or more cultures interact. The idea has been used "as a lens by citizens of former colonies and their opportunities to redefine the boundaries of their own lives" and by Muslim women from conservative backgrounds who have reimagined a life in the American culture.

When available reality and accompanying vocabulary, voices, experiences, and even identities fail us, a third space helps us imagine the future in an almost revolutionary manner.

Kirsi LaPointe and Elina Henttonen have long careers as researchers and teachers of leadership and organizational development. "We loved our jobs but began to feel less satisfied in the academic environment where quotas and competitiveness became the most important goals," they state. "We saw cultures that stagnated on a continuum of overemphasis on individual performance to seeing employees as a simple cog in the wheel."

They propose that instead of assuming all new ideas must fit in the confines of existing space, people take over a *new* space in organizational design. So instead of squeezing women's priorities and goals inside structures built by men, women can design what they want and need from organizations outside current boundaries.

LaPointe and Henttonen's research imagines a third space organizational culture that goes beyond individual performance and managerialism. In that third space the employee is seen and respected as an individual. People are not asked to downplay what is unique about them—their abilities, gender, race, national origin, or age—but these things are fully at play. Intersectionality, along with individual experiences and capabilities, is considered central when an organization is looking to reimagine new ways of being. In fact, organizational redesign is impossible without these voices and experiences at the table.

An organization that begins to question its design and culture invites new voices in the redesign. This includes the recognition that people make decisions by drawing on their cultural backgrounds and taking advantage of that. This is a strengths-based approach to diversity and incorporates people's perspectives into all work of the organization, as opposed to niche areas or representation (think Latinx employees contributing to campaigns for Latinx audiences). The organization begins to rethink markets, products, strategies, missions, business practices, and even cultures as seen through the eyes of diverse team members.

There is no more opportune time to start thinking about organizational practices through the eyes of women than in our shared post-Covid-19 reality. Women's experiences during the pandemic were disproportionately challenging and so seems to be their post-Covid world consequently. Ideas about how women would like to reimagine work can offer missional organizations with useful and innovative building blocks for a third space reality.

Work sharing. In a complex world, the work of teams is more important than the heroic achievements of individual employees. Relying on the talent of the "star employee" leads to burnout, one-size-fits-all products, and slowdown of what can be accomplished. Working on teams where several people contribute to the end product not only makes the work more innovative, it also creates a work culture that is sustainable for people in different life stages. Successful work sharing relies on three key investments: hiring team members who are reliable and deliver their results on time, investment by organizations in managers who know how to lead teams and understand team dynamics, and rewarding teams over individuals.

We've often seen diverse teams assign credit to "those who need it the most." Let's face it: a leader may not need credit for a job well done or to add their name to a published article, but for a more junior member, those accolades may be career-changing. Managers who lead teams well can make these decisions with a generous hand.

The office. We recently talked to a colleague who rented a second apartment in the DC suburbs because his new missional organization required him to relocate. This feels shocking in the post-Covid environment. Yes, gathering in offices will continue to serve a purpose in the workplace. Some of the shared cultures, symbols, and rituals that take place in a physical space cannot be replicated virtually. But in the future, gathering in offices should be used strategically—for team building, vision casting, and getting to know staff who live across states and even oceans from each other. For many women the ability to work virtually has offered a significant relief from the stresses of daily life—grooming, commuting, the office drama that can eat hours from a day—and they do not want to return to the old structures of daily office work.

Virtual success. Google's Project Aristotle study identified three levers that predicted a team's cohesion during the transition to virtual work brought about by Covid-19. First was leveraging new technologies like Zoom and Teams. For example, the private chat functions in virtual platforms enabled managers to nudge individual (more timid) employees to speak up. Second was the design of new rituals in the online format. Virtual work abolished ad hoc conversations in the office, instead teams that were able to establish strong mechanisms for connecting online experienced stronger connection. Finally, Covid-19 gave us a shared opportunity to show compassion and care. Because everyone was experiencing the same difficulties together, it was easier to speak about hard things out loud and share in each other's struggles. Missional organizations benefited from the opportunity to come together in weekly prayer and bringing our cares collectively to God. What a privilege. Additionally, as Arianna Huffington shares in a blog post, "Hard skills and expertise are always going to be table stakes, but to successfully navigate the new hybrid world defined by changing routines and continuing uncertainty we'll need human skills—empathy, resilience, collaboration, team building and creativity." Skills that we would call "feminine."

Questioning the eight-hour workday. The ecosystem of the nine-to-five has broken down during the pandemic. Now organizations have the challenge of evaluating what value a return to a strict forty-hour week would have for productivity and quality of work or whether they could adapt more flexible and adaptable work hours. Missional organizations could take a critical look at productivity and how much it would actually fall if individuals were able to self-direct their work and had autonomy to set their own hours. We spoke previously about women benefiting from work that is targeted and well-defined. In such an environment it would seem realistic for people to also define the amount of time their work requires.

WHAT MEN HAVE LEARNED

We spoke to three men whose wives hold high-level positions in missional organizations. In this crucial conversation about shared leadership between women and men, it is important to hear what men have learned as their partners have flourished in their careers and organizations. These men, many of whom have supported their wives' careers over decades, have forged a path against the norm, and it has not always been easy. Their stories offer many valuable takeaways about supporting women inside organizations. Sachin Louis speaks to us about his wife, Anu, CEO of an organization in Canada:

> I was an established executive in the IT industry in India when I met Anu and when we married. Though I was raised in a traditional household, where gender roles were prescribed by Indian culture, and educated in an all-boys private school, my sister and I were both encouraged to become anything we wanted when we grew up. My church taught traditional theology against women preaching, and at university there were only twenty female students out of over three hundred in my field of study. It wasn't until I worked with a large international for-profit that I experienced women and men in the same leadership roles and where I first reported to a female leader. I admired and respected her inclusive leadership style and that began to develop my mindset toward women in senior roles.
>
> To support my wife's significant new leadership role and the upcoming birth of our twins, I relocated to Canada, where Anu's new role was based. I also stepped out of my profession for a time to be the primary caregiver to our girls.

After I heard Anu speak at a conference of the work she was doing to rescue girls from human trafficking, and the physical challenges she herself has faced in her work, I knew that if she felt even 1 percent inclined to take on this new role, I would agree.

Dan and Michele Rickett both work for a women's freedom and empowerment organization, Dan as the vice president for programs and Michele as CEO. Dan shares his experience with us:

I was raised in a home where my parents had traditional gender roles—my father as the head of the household. In my career over the past four decades, I formed and led numerous organizations in the missional sector and served under several female leaders with different qualities and giftings. Michele and I "grew up together" and I was long aware that Michele would and should come into her own calling and I prayed for that day. When our organization emerged from another organization, it was Michele's vision and would be her leadership role.

It makes a world of difference that Christ has always been at the center of our relationship. In forty-seven years of marriage, serious conflict has been rare and always settled by apology, forgiveness, and forbearance. We brought those behaviors into our workplace relationship. While I report to the board chair, having your wife as your CEO isn't without some struggles.

The challenges we've faced are due to differences in leadership style and expectations early on. I expected to advise Michele on matters of organization and leadership. I had decades of experience in organizational leadership, and I was a competent consultant on the subject. Michele didn't appreciate my intrusion into her role as founder and CEO. I was making the mistake of offering advice when it wasn't asked for. To be honest, I wouldn't have appreciated it had she intruded the same way in my role over international programs.

Our occasional differences of opinion and sometimes of style created friction in executive team meetings. Even if my usual style is to challenge the CEO when needed, I couldn't do that with Michele. The responsibility was on me to become more trusting and diplomatic. Though other men never said a word, I occasionally saw the look of disapproval—of a husband working under the authority of his wife. I could hear them thinking, "He must be the follower, not the leader," or "'Michele is the strong one in their marriage." It didn't shake my confidence. Those thoughts would never cross the minds of men who know me.

Finally, Harold Overstreet's wife, Jane, is the CEO of an international educational organization. Harold is retired from leadership roles for major missional organizations. Though raised by parents who had traditional gender roles, his father traveled a lot and left his mother as the head of the household on day-to-day matters. Harold shares this with us:

I came to understand God's call for women in leadership both through the female pastor at my Methodist church growing up and through the impact of Jane's father during my teenage years. Seeing how he treated Jane with such an "of course she can do that" attitude probably had more influence than anything else. I just saw him making room for women in everything he did. And so, from the beginning, Jane was out doing the same things I was doing.

In the long run it meant a lot of confirmation and affirmation of the clear call to leadership for Jane. It meant my role was the one who handled things around the house and caring for our children as Jane traveled quite a bit for work. It wasn't always easy.

I recall moments of thinking, "My wife is flourishing and I'm not." But the Lord got ahold of me and said, "You've got time with your kids you'll never have again. You've got the time to spend with them and invest in them." Once I realized that, I began getting really involved in their baseball leagues and other activities. Once I embraced my part, I never looked back. We've realized over our forty years of marriage, there's been seasons of "This is my time" and "This is Jane's time," and we've gone back and forth on that over the years. The result of all of this is also three grown children who are walking with the Lord, happily married, and thriving in their respective lives.

● ● ●

Reimagining a space where women can flourish beyond the workplace takes the imagination of both women and men. We can shake the expectations societal norms force on us—perfectionism, not asking for help, expressing ambition—in our own terms. All these are needed for women to carve out their own roles in missional organizations. Finally, both men and women play a role in reimagining a "third space" in organizations and families. This space is often countercultural and takes a stand against the expectations of existing communities, families, and organizations. But brave men and women embrace this space for a better shared future.

Belonging organizations can support women beyond the workplace by

- taking inventory of how unpaid care work shows up in their organizational context,
- thinking of ways women and men inside organizations can overcome society's expectations by centering Sabbath, focusing on excellence over expansion, and slowing down for the last and the least to catch up,
- and learning from the ways women and men have defined a third space for themselves in various life situations.

CONCLUSION

We have created a D&I role and advisory council. The organization is working with female leaders to gain flex roles and responsibilities, hours, and location to manage their personal demands. We are investing in a post-pandemic remote-friendly work environment."

"All staff are doing a Bible study series on women and men leading together. The organization is engaging in conversations at all levels around gender equality and it is very encouraging."

"Our organization has created a more inclusive culture for women by simply honoring them and giving them equal opportunities to men. For example, our organization recently provided childcare for nursing mothers with children less than six months old on a retreat out of state."

"We initiated a mothers' mentorship program that invites expectant women on staff to be paired with another working mom mentor during her pregnancy and first year postpartum."

"I am seeing a lot of political will around pursuing and investing in diversity, inclusion, and equity, with emphasis on gender. This includes defining and socializing a theologically based statement on gender equality and placing it firmly in the organizational values and affirmations."

In the process of interviewing for this book, we spoke to dozens of women and men working in missional organizations. Much of what they had to say was discouraging at best, heartbreaking at worst. The gap between where we are and where we need to be is disheartening. Still, those we spoke to were quick to acknowledge it when their organization was taking positive steps toward a culture of belonging. Most organizations can tell similar stories of efforts, no matter how imperfect and sometimes short-lived. These efforts are the seeds that can grow into mainstreamed organizational strategy. A systemic approach to creating a culture of belonging builds on the many valuable things already taking place across our sector, if organizations continue the investment.

We have proposed that organizations pull on all available levers to create the new culture missional organizations need to face future challenges. This includes engaging questions such as:

- Have we examined the leadership and organizational culture for what accepted leadership behavior looks like and thus what is expected of anyone who wants to be in leadership?

- Do we investigate our theological beliefs and cultural practices and how they can hinder women's flourishing?

- What are the human resource policies and practices that may be obstructing us from creating the diverse cultures we are looking for?

- Have we developed people in the organization to adopt this new way of thinking and being together, including creating spaces for women to level the playing field?

Sometimes these problems seem too great to resolve. We've talked to many leaders who dream of executing a brand-new organization, starting with a clean slate, and building from scratch. This might be the easier way forward, but it's not what we're collectively called to. We believe we are called to be change agents and move our long-established missional organizations into a new era of reflecting the kingdom of God. The work of belonging is not a shortcut that avoids chaos and discomfort. The work starts with facing chaos and discomfort. It starts with reconciliation.

COMPASSIONATE LISTENING

Michele is a facilitator who works with women and men in gender equity and reconciliation. "I bought into patriarchy early in my life," she tells us. "I felt that I was complicit in many ways. Because I accepted that as a young woman, everything was harder for me. It was harder to be taken seriously and have my voice heard, and in the corporate world no matter what I did, men would just patronize me or hit on me. I thought this was just the way things were.

"But when my spiritual journey expanded, I became uncomfortable with the environment I was working in," Michele continues.

> Instead I became interested in the work of gender reconciliation and dialogue between women and men. I realized that if we are to have a conversation about women's empowerment, we need to bring men into the conversation. I realized that it's not just women who are in pain; men too bear wounds as a result of being stereotyped and trying to fit the image of who they're supposed to be. Men have spent years hearing, "Don't cry," or, "Man up." The aha moment for me was when women and men came into the same room and shared their stories and engaged in deep, compassionate listening. They shared how cultural stereotypes have shaped their lives, and also how they have each felt wounded by them. I realized that if we can hold each other's stories with compassion and without judgment, people can begin to heal. And there is a difference between understanding the harm intellectually and experiencing healing in your heart. My own heart started to expand when I heard these stories from both men and women. So I've come to believe strongly that we all need healing and reconciliation before we can become change agents in our communities and organizations.

"We have a long way to go," Michele concludes.

> When I travel, I hear stories of the marriages of twelve- to thirteen-year-old girls, or the violence women are subjected to in their own homes, for something as minor as "burning the food." I also hear the stories of talented women who are not taken as seriously as they should be in their workplace, because they choose to put career ahead of family and remain unmarried. I speak often to my students about the parable of the talents and the obedience required of us as Christians to explore and use our gifts for building the kingdom. And how men, by not allowing women to have a voice, are actually complicit in obstructing women from being obedient to God in using their talents.

Reconciliation between women and men starts with listening in safe spaces and letting the story of the other break your heart. As a male colleague who recently participated in a forum on gender shared, "After each woman spoke, the men's mouths dropped as they realized they had witnessed subjugation of women all their lives and had not been aware of it. They had systematically or structurally participated in the dismissal of the image of God in their sisters. And they had been party to injustice, even while working for justice."

This practice and experience of deep truth-telling requires empathy, vulnerability, and transparency. Listening and hearing can create a shared space for heartfelt lament. We lament the God-given talents, opportunities, time, and resources that are left unused in kingdom work. We lament the abuse and pain this wasted talent has caused women. We lament the misunderstandings that have held not just women but men back from living in the fullness of God's beautiful calling.

An integral part of shared learning is also the discovery of new ways of being rooted in mutual appreciation, compassion, and trust. This is when women and men envision together what could be and begin to build a shared community around it. These communities are committed to acknowledging not only pain and the need for healing, but also the need to transform gender relations. In these communities, we must develop tools and frameworks, including policies and practices, communication skills, and the ability to work through conflict together.

WHAT'S IT GOING TO COST ME?

Organizational cultures are born in the intersections of shared relationships. If the quality of those relationships is healthy and constructive, that's the kind of culture we'll experience. If those relationships are toxic and fear-filled, well, that's exactly the culture we'll bear witness to. Cultures of belonging are built on the belief that the relationships within our organization can be healed and so can our organizational cultures. This healing depends not just on reconciliation between people inside our organizations *now* but also on examining who has been left out. To share kingdom relationships, no one can be left out of the equation.

What does this mean to each of us individually?

We must examine how we have personally benefited from unhealthy relationships and why we haven't done our part to shake the status quo. This painful reality manifests in different ways. It may mean not speaking up when a colleague's performance comes off in an unfavorable light but makes mine look good. It may mean withholding opportunities from people who are not deemed a "culture fit" for fear of disturbing the peace or because of personal prejudices. It may mean buying into dominant gender roles that presume women aren't fit to lead. It may mean fear of sharing our platform or even giving it up for someone whose voice is needed in the next chapter of the organization. None of us is exempt from thinking this way. We're all wired for self-preservation and getting the most out of opportunities, even in ways that are antithetical to our faith. So we must ask, "What does it mean for me? What might I have to give up? What is it going to cost me?"

When a large missional organization was implementing a gender equality initiative, many of the men interviewed began their feedback with, "Why are we doing this?" One said, "Before discussing strategies, it would be helpful to understand the real 'why' and if this is a broad concern or only a concern of a small number of people 'echoed by two others.'" Another asked, "Why are we focusing on women so much? We've heard the stats, but why should we do this?" The same organizational review exposed massive problems with how women were treated and the lack of opportunities they experienced.

The reality is, those who benefit from the status quo rarely notice how it holds others back. They are like these brothers who don't even think there *is* a problem, let alone want to join in finding a solution. These are not the voices that should be leading the conversation.

Those currently in leadership roles in the missional sector may think they should be the ones finding solutions for the decades to come. But this is the cost: many missional organizations need brand-new leadership. Organizations and senior leaders who are serious about culture shift are beginning to center minoritized voices. We see this happening through practical steps such as committing publicly to diversity in the recruitment of new leaders, aggressively targeting women and minority candidates in hiring, and having very transparent and public conversations about selection criteria. Most importantly, this is happening with senior male leaders voluntarily writing themselves out of the script.

For this mindset change, we start at the start: Who should presume that they'll be in leadership someday? In the shared leadership model we propose here, it should be everyone and anyone, but with a caveat. As we collectively seek for the most talented, forward-looking, and innovative leaders, we must train our eyes and ears to identify that type of leadership in new individuals and groups. Missional organizations will not find the next generation of leaders by looking in the mirror. They will find them serving and being served through our programs and services, as well as in the pipelines of the next generations across the sector.

We invite those who benefit because of gender or race to dig deep and re-imagine an organization where more people who don't look like them can thrive. It's an invitation to advocate for leveling the playing field. To intentionally make space in organizations for women and colleagues of color to have greater influence. The cost may be a shift in your role, your leadership expanse, perhaps even your standing in the organization. When the next opportunity arises for you to expand your influence, it may mean that you instead extend that opportunity to someone else.

WHAT IS OUR LEGACY?

There is no greater legacy than the building up of people. I (Beth) have spent my career developing thousands of leaders in the missional sector, and this is what I have seen: when you invest in people, it creates a legacy that can't be taken away from you. It can't be swept away with the next earthquake, national or international political turmoil, or economic downturn.

It's time to rethink how we define legacy. Many organizational leaders want to do good in the world. They make statements like, "We're going to double the annual number of houses we build," or, "We're going to increase our water installations by 400 percent in the next two years," or, "We're going to expand our child development programs to four new countries." These are all worthy and good things. The need for the work of missional organizations continues to be great in the world. And as long as we're not trampling on the communities we serve by growing too aggressively or burning out our staff by expecting double workload and no new resources, these are noble goals.

But if success in our sector is measured only by more, bigger, and better, we are missing out on celebrating the work God is doing in the midst of loyal staff, in the margins where small innovations are being birthed, and among leaders and staff who show up every day through faithful and excellent work. The miracle we pray for is not just the big, next thing *out there*; it is the constant, relentless, humble work *in here.*

The culture that seeks growth and shiny new things at any cost, even that of cultural and leadership health, is at risk of an unhealthy leadership legacy. The fall of many great missional leaders in the past decades speaks to organizational cultures that valued growth and celebrity above all else without proper checks and balances on individual leadership styles.

Boards, executive teams, and donors are as responsible as the leaders who fell. What was given premium value behind closed doors? Did the culture celebrate the bottom line more than cultural health? The mighty dollar over the widow's mite? Did executive teams see more unchecked power the higher the organization tracked? Does our sector claim to care for the last and the least but compete instead for the highest growth rate or the brightest reputation?

Jesus showed us a better way through his ministry, and it's not to pursue "more ministry" to secure our own legacy. For too long we have accepted and even pursued the broken practices of this world within our organizations, reflecting the marred identity of success at the expense of our identity as God's beloved. No tiny amount of organizational success—and it is all tiny in his eyes—will ever have greater value than our work in ushering in the shalom of the kingdom.

Good for business and good for people must exist in the same framework—no doubt about that.

Why else would the Scriptures promise that we would be equipped "with every good thing to do his will" (Hebrews 13:21)? Our organizations are meant to be places of prosperity and resources for the work we are called to. They are also meant to be communities of belonging. Let's not sacrifice any longer the belonging our people could experience on the altar of our own personal legacy.

TO FUTURE LEADERS

In the words of the psalmist, "I praise you, for I am fearfully and wonderfully made. Wonderful are your works; my soul knows it very well" (Psalm 139:14 ESV). For decades, the counsel we've received as women is to change ourselves. In church communities we must be modest, compliant, and quiet. As mothers we must turn off our own ambition and talent. As leaders we must turn on assertiveness and charisma. We learn to hide away and downplay the truest parts of ourselves to make others more comfortable. Many spaces women turn up in feel unfamiliar and unwelcoming because we're asked to change so much about ourselves to fit in.

But if God wanted us all to parent and lead the same way, wouldn't he have made us more like an army than the motley crew of "fearfully and wonderfully made" creatures we are?

Midcentury feminist Simone de Beauvoir states, "It is in the knowledge of the genuine conditions of our lives that [women] must draw our strength to live and our reasons for acting." In other words, the places we come from— the intersections of identity, our socioeconomic backgrounds, our level of education, our life situation and that of those we care for, even the trauma we have walked through—all must inform how and why we work and lead. Those unique things, the genuine conditions of our lives, are what make our contributions in organizations so unique and needed.

We spoke with Sharon, who describes her family's return to Rwanda from exile when she was eight years old. "It was a few months after the genocide; they were still cleaning the streets. Rwanda had lost many men to the war, so it was the women who went right to work, and my mother put me in school," Sharon remembers.

> There was a lot of female energy in the rebuilding of Rwanda. It was the birth of a new kind of Rwandan woman, a woman who had a platform and a place in the society. In college I saw examples of women, even young women, speaking their mind and rising to leadership positions. The country saw the numbers of women in the Parliament increase and there was an overall mentality that women *must* be a part of the rebuilding process. This need overtook personal preferences and opinions in the society. It overcame the voices of men who believed that women needed to remain restricted to traditional female roles.

Sharon concludes, "Women in Rwanda were needed in rebuilding. I saw women work past their trauma and loss and rise to leadership. The thing my country got right was to give those women a platform."

In Rwanda, women could not wait to be ready or have their circumstances be perfect so they could contribute. They needed to participate from where they were standing. Jacqueline, a finance director for an international NGO, says of her country's progress, "Rwanda today is so different from Rwanda in 1994. Development and education have improved. Investment in youth and capacity-building initiatives have grown. Women have been lifted up and their contributions to the development of the country have been noticed." The impact of Rwandese women has been significant.

Like the women in Rwanda, we as women are called to leadership now. We cannot wait for our circumstances to get better or for our organizations to improve.

We know. This is a lot to ask.

Many women working in the missional sector are disillusioned by decades of service and very little progress. Women have stuck their neck out for a cause only to experience reckoning in the next round of cuts or opportunities for advancement. Others have been burned by bosses and cultures that have not accepted their life circumstances or cultural identities. Yet others experience burnout resulting from inflexibility, overwork, and under pay.

It's a lot to ask from women to stick around for a good fight.

So instead of asking you to stick around and put up with "same old, same old," we propose that you join a movement of women and men allies who are serious about creating change in our sector. These women and men are all around us—perhaps hiding in your own organization, looking for *you* to partner with them on this great cause. And then you must . . .

Lead from who you are. We have discussed the many ways women are needed in organizations just as they are. Our leadership styles, empathy, and ability to understand the needs of women and families our organizations serve across the world are just some of the unique talents we bring to the table. Your leadership style may be analytical, assertive, or charismatic. All of these are needed. The greatest value you bring to the table as a leader is understanding your unique gifts and talents and how they can serve the organization and the sector and learn to *lean into them*. You may say to us, "That's what I did before, and they didn't like it." Which brings us to the next point.

Relentlessly look for organizations that share your values. We have seen women flounder in certain roles or organizations turn around and flourish somewhere else. The biggest lie we believe is that "there is something wrong with me." There is nothing wrong with you—you just haven't found the boss, the team, or the organization that appreciates what you have to bring. If you are miserable where you are serving, keep looking for a place where you can belong. Now, we understand the privilege in that statement: many women are not able to give up a job, no matter how miserable. Many of us need income, health insurance, and stability. Still, keep looking. Make sure people in the sector know you are looking for opportunities; learn to speak openly about your skills and abilities; and never, ever believe the lie that there is something wrong with you.

Build a bigger table. Women need bigger tables for several reasons. As we've explored, there aren't enough women leaders in the sector to create change—that is, if we remain siloed. If women across organizations decide to come together to pool their voices and resources, much can be established. We need combined resources to get better data on the sector, to establish Rolodexes of women who can serve as executives and on boards, and to advocate for key issues that matter to us collectively. Women should not be afraid to join their voices in this way; men have done it for decades. Women need bigger tables that allow them to network and keep an eye on emerging talent across organizations. Women have the capacity to be proponents for each other on teams and projects, and networks give us the ability to connect with each other to know "who's out there."

Extend your hand to others. If and when you become someone of influence and impact in your organization, become a role model for advocating on the behalf of others and lifting them up. Don't believe the lie that the pie is finite and once you have a slice, you have to protect it with your life. Instead, decide to generously share what you have with others.

It is time to forsake the old, outdated models of leadership where there is no room to expand. The time for leadership expansion—of hearts and postures, for women and men—is now.

ACKNOWLEDGMENTS

D r. Beth Birmingham: I'm grateful to Jane Overstreet, David Fraser, and Jim Engel and our time in The Center for Organizational Excellence at Eastern College (now University) for showing me early in my career what a belonging culture and shared leadership could look like and modeling godly leadership for all who follow.

Eeva Sallinen Simard: I thank all of the excellent bosses I've had. Each of you has taught me something unique about leadership: Brian Lange, Peter Taggart, Joe Agostino, Jennifer Bryce, Stephan Bauman, Oying Rimon, Tim Breene, Scott Arbeiter, Kathleen Leslie, Myal Greene, Lanre Williams-Ayedun. I also thank my family: Muori Leena Rihu, Äiti Kaija Canino, Iskä Tuomas Sallinen, Anna Braganza, Ruut DeMeo, Saara Sallinen, and my loves: Amelie, Tuomas, and Rene.

The authors would like to acknowledge the valuable contributions to this book project by Dr. Mimi Haddad, Dr. Amy Reynolds, Sarah Brackbill-Jackson, Kati Shepardson, and Amethyst A. Rodriguez. They helped by reviewing drafts, formatting text, and offering views for early work. The authors would also like to thank Elissa Schauer, Rachel Hastings, Ed Gilbreath, and the entire team at InterVarsity Press. The authors would like to thank the women and men who agreed to be interviewed for this book, including in focus groups and the following individuals: Katherine Marshall, Sandra Van Opstal, Renee Blanding, Craig Stewart, Prabu Deepan, Christina Klinepeter, Jenny Yang, Amy McCullough, Sachin Louis, Dan Rickett, Harold Overstreet, Michele Breene, and Sharon Greene.

THE BELONGING CULTURE
FRAMEWORK SUMMARY

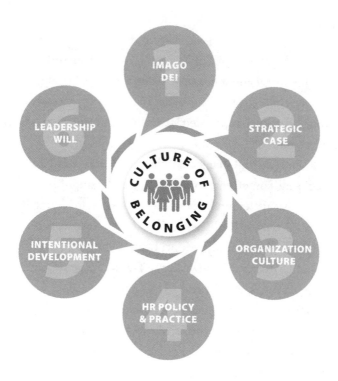

Perhaps your organization has tried to create a more diverse organization but has been frustrated when those efforts came up short. We present this model as necessary in addressing the whole system of your organization to create space for underrepresented voices, whether that is women, BIPOC leaders, or people of different nationalities.

IMAGO DEI

First and throughout the process, becoming a belonging culture requires that we see the image of God in each other. Men need to see and recognize that God made women in his image and for his purposes and gifted them for that calling. Those gifts include leadership, preaching, and teaching.

Women need to see the image of God in the men who have hurt them and marginalized them. It's too easy to demonize a man who doesn't know any better, who has been socialized in wrong beliefs about women and hasn't been held accountable until now for bad behaviors. To borrow the title of Bishop Tutu's book, there is no future without forgiveness.

STRATEGIC CASE

While it offends many women that this is required, it has taken "the strategic case" as a point to convince leaders that creating more diverse leadership and highlighting the influence of women is good for the organization and its performance outcomes. And there's research to support that reality. Significant representation of women in leadership (35 percent or more) is not a "nice to have" but a strategic necessity.

ORGANIZATIONAL CULTURE

You can see the image of God in each other, you can make the strategic case for why change is necessary, but if you don't tackle the organizational cultures that were originally created by men to welcome only men, you will see women "check out" either emotionally or physically from your organization, exacerbating the likelihood that you'll be able to recruit any in the future. How is performance measured, who gets celebrated, what toxic behaviors are supported or ignored for the sake of "more and better" ministry?

HUMAN RESOURCE POLICIES AND PRACTICES

From throwing the recruiting net to celebrating the exit and retirement of employees, there's bias in the system that embraces male behaviors and diminishes women's behaviors. This shows up in how women show up in interviews, views of what "leadership track material" looks like, and how women are judged for aggressively promoting themselves and negotiating raises, when those are expected of men. We can see each other as the image of God, understand the business case, and begin to address culture, but if HR practices and policies aren't examined from beginning to end, the movement of the culture will be much harder.

INTENTIONAL DEVELOPMENT

Even if all of these previous levers have been pushed, perhaps your organization has spent decades favoring the development of men over women when it comes to leadership and influence. Perhaps the message you've given is that women need to "show up" more like men—until they do and are admonished for it. A culture of belonging needs to intentionally develop everyone if it is going to rewrite the curriculum scripts on what good leadership and influence look like. Women too need to overcome mental hurdles by believing that the way God has equipped them for leadership *is* leadership. Not a mistake, not an accident. They are his beloved, called for his purposes, and equipped for his work.

LEADERSHIP WILL

This lever is actually first and last. None of these changes will be implemented unless existing leaders have the courage and the will to recognize the image of God they have diminished in women, the strategic case for better performance of their organization, and understanding that the whole organizational system has been working against a belonging culture all along. Systems can be changed. But this requires much more than a heartwarming public statement of affirming diversity. It requires the backbone to start and stay the course to see it through to bearing fruit.

Does all this feel like too much? It shouldn't. In our combined thirty-plus years in the sector, we have watched far more ambitious "global change" agendas executed in missional organizations with far fewer necessary outcomes. Creating a belonging culture will be the legacy you leave because it will forever change the positive outcomes of your organization. Everything else you do for the success of your organization and the communities you serve will pale in comparison to this endeavor.

SUGGESTED READING

LEADERSHIP RESOURCES FROM WOMEN OF COLOR

Banaji, Mahzarin R. and Anthony G. Greenwald. *Blindspot: Hidden Biases of Good People*. New York: Delacorte Press, 2013.

Bordas, Juana. *The Power of Latino Leadership: Culture, Inclusion, and Contribution*. Oakland, CA: Berrett-Koehler Publishers, 2013.

Brown, Austin Channing. *I'm Still Here: Black Dignity in a World Made for Whiteness*. New York: Convergent Books, 2018.

Cleveland, Christena. *Disunity in Christ: Uncovering the Hidden Forces that Keep Us Apart*. Downers Grove, IL: InterVarsity Press, 2013.

Eberhardt, Jennifer L. *Biased: Uncovering the Hidden Prejudice That Shapes What We See, Think, and Do*. New York: Viking, 2019.

Harper, Lisa Sharon. *The Very Good Gospel: How Everything Wrong Can Be Made Right*. Colorado Springs: WaterBrook, 2016.

Harts, Minda. *The Memo: What Women of Color Need to Know to Secure a Seat at the Table*. New York: Seal Press, 2020.

———. *Right Within: How to Heal from Racial Trauma in the Workplace*. New York: Seal Press, 2021.

Ngunjiri, Faith Wambura. *Women's Spiritual Leadership in Africa: Tempered Radicals and Critical Servant Leaders*. Albany, NY: SUNY Press, 2010.

Parker, Priya. *The Art of Gathering: How We Meet and Why It Matters*. New York: Riverhead Books, 2018.

Saujani, Reshma. *Pay Up: The Future of Women and Work (and Why It's Different Than You Think)*. New York: Atria/One Signal Publishers, 2022.

GENDER PROGRAMMING

Avakyan, Yeva, Keshet Bachan, Valerie Rhoe Davis, Kelly Fish, Christie Getman, Laura Romah, Meredith Saggers, Kristi Tabaj, Jenn Williamson, and Elise Young. *Minimum Standards for Mainstreaming Gender Equality*. Gender Practitioners Collaborative, accessed April 5, 2022. https://genderstandards.org.

Deepan, Prabu. *Transforming Masculinities*. Teddington, England: Tearfund, 2017. https://learn.tearfund.org/en/resources/tools-and-guides/transforming-masculinities.

Nkonya, Leticia, Jacqueline Ogega, Godfrey Senkaba, Edward Winter, and Zayid Douglas. *Manual for Trainers and Facilitators: Gender Equality and Social Inclusion*. World Vision,

August 2021. www.worldvision.org/wp-content/uploads/2021/10/GESI-DME-Training -Manual.pdf.

United Nations Population Fund and United Nations Development Fund for Women. *Gender Responsive Budgeting in Practice*. New York: United Nations Population Fund, 2006. https:// unfpa.org/sites/default/files/pub-pdf/gender_manual_eng.pdf.

PREVENTION OF SEXUAL EXPLOITATION AND ASSAULT

Basile, Kathleen C., Sarah DeGue, Kathryn Jones, Kimberley Freire, Jenny Dills, Sharon G. Smith, and Jerris L. Raiford. *Stop CV: A Technical Package to Prevent Sexual Violence*. Atlanta: Division of Violence Prevention, National Center for Injury Prevention and Control, Centers for Disease Control and Prevention, 2016. www.cdc.gov/violenceprevention/pdf /SV-Prevention-Technical-Package.pdf.

InterAction. *Prevention of Sexual Exploitation and Abuse of Beneficiaries* Online Training. Accessed April 5, 2022. www.interaction.org/training/.

UNICEF. *Prevention of Sexual Exploitation and Assault* Online Training. Accessed April 5, 2022. https://agora.unicef.org/course/info.php?id=7380.

United Nations Office for the Coordination of Humanitarian Affairs. *Standard Operating Procedures on Sexual Misconduct: Protection from Sexual Exploitation and Abuse and Sexual Harassment*. New York: United Nations OCHA, March 2021. www.unocha.org/sites/unocha /files/OCHA_SoP_Sexual_Misconduct_EN_07072021.pdf.

THEOLOGICAL GENDER EQUALITY

Barr, Beth Allison. *The Making of Biblical Womanhood: How the Subjugation of Women Became Gospel Truth*. Grand Rapids, MI: Brazos Press, 2021.

Beaty, Katelyn. *A Woman's Place: Christian Vision for Your Calling in the Office, the Home, and the World*. Brentwood, TN: Howard Books, 2016.

Bessey, Sarah. *Jesus Feminist: An Invitation to Revisit the Bible's View of Women*. Brentwood, TN: Howard Books, 2013.

Christians for Biblical Equality. Online resources. www.cbeinternational.org/.

Cunningham, Loren, and David Joel Hamilton. *Why Not Women: A Fresh Look at Scripture on Women in Missions, Ministry and Leadership*. Seattle, WA: YWAM Publishing, 2000.

Development Associates International. *Women and Men Serving Together Training*. Gleneagle, CO: Development Associates International, 2020. https://institute.daintl.org/courses /women-and-men-serving-together/.

Lederleitner, Mary T. *Women in God's Mission: Accepting the Invitation to Serve and Lead*. Downers Grove, IL: InterVarsity Press 2018.

Porter King, Jeanne. *Leading Lessons: Insights on Leadership from Women of the Bible*. Minneapolis, MN: Fortress Press, 2005.

ADDITIONAL LEADERSHIP READING

Ammerman, Colleen, and Boris Groysberg. *Glass Half Broken: Shattering the Barriers That Still Hold Women Back at Work*. Boston: Harvard Business Review Press, 2021.

Brown, Brené. *Dare to Lead: Brave Work. Tough Conversations. Whole Hearts*. New York: Random House, 2016.

Carter, Jimmy. *A Call to Action: Women, Religion, Violence and Power*. New York: Simon & Schuster, 2014.

Criado Perez, Caroline. *Invisible Women: Data Bias in a World Designed for Men*. New York: Harry N. Abrams Publishing, 2016.

Du Mez, Kristin Kobes. *Jesus and John Wayne: How White Evangelicals Corrupted a Faith and Fractured a Nation*. New York: Liveright Publishing, 2020.

Eagly, Alice H. and Linda L. Carli. *Through the Labyrinth: The Truth About How Women Become Leaders*. Boston: Harvard Business Review Press, 2007.

Gates, Melinda. *The Moment of Lift: How Empowering Women Changes the World*. New York: Flatiron Books, 2019.

Ngunjiri, Faith Wambura, Karen A. Longman, and Cynthia Cherrey, eds. *Women and Leadership Around the World*. Charlotte, NC: Information Age Publishing, Inc., 2015.

NOTES

1. THE MISSIONAL ORGANIZATION HAS A PROBLEM WITH WOMEN

12   *Faith-based organizations*: Juul Peterson, "International Religious NGOs at The United Nations: A Study of a Group of Religious Organizations," *The Journal of Humanitarian Assistance*, November 17, 2010, sites.tufts.edu/jha/archives/847.

14   *In the United States*: Brice S. McKeever, "The Nonprofit Sector in Brief 2018: Public Charities, Giving, and Volunteering," Urban Institute, December 13, 2018, nccs.urban .org/publication/nonprofit-sector-brief-2018.
   According to GuideStar: "Directory of Charities and Nonprofit Organizations," Guide-Star, copyright 2022, www.guidestar.org/NonprofitDirectory.aspx.
   Through the 1980s: Interview with Katherine Marshall, executive director of World Faiths Development Dialogue, July 9, 2021.

15   *Challenged by books*: William Russell Easterly, *The White Man's Burden: Why the West's Efforts to Aid the Rest Have Done So Much Ill and So Little Good* (New York: Penguin, 2006); Steve Corbett and Brian Fikkert, *When Helping Hurts: How to Alleviate Poverty Without Hurting the Poor. . . . and Yourself* (Chicago: Moody Publishers, 2014); *Poverty, Inc.*, directed by Michael Matheson Miller, written by Michael Matheson Miller, Simon Scionka, and Jonathan Witt (2014; Passion River).

16   *Women make up*: Young-Joo Lee, "Male Nonprofit CEOs Earn More—but the Problem Runs Deeper than a Simple Gender Pay Gap," The Conversation," July 2, 2019, theconversation.com/male-nonprofit-ceos-earn-more-but-the-problem-runs-deeper -than-a-simple-gender-pay-gap-119068.
   A Gordon College study: Amy Reynolds and Janel Curry, "Best Practices for Attracting, Promoting, and Retaining Female Leadership in Christian Organizations," Report for the Women in Leadership National Study, Gordon College, January 2017.

17   *Figure 1*: Amy Reynolds and Janel Curry, "Best Practices for Attracting, Promoting, and Retaining Female Leadership in Christian Organizations," Report for the Women in Leadership National Study, Gordon College, January 2017.

18   *A recent analysis*: Alice H Eagly, Mona G. Makhijani, Bruce G. Klonsky, "Gender and the Evaluation of Leaders: A Meta-Analysis," *Psychological Bulletin* 111, no. 1 (January 1992): 3-22.
   There is this prime: Ama Marston, "Women in Leadership: 'It's Not Going to Work the Way We're Doing It,'" *The Guardian*, August 1, 2013, www.theguardian.com/global -development-professionals-network/2013/aug/01/women-in-leadership-inter national-ngos.

20   *"There has always been"*: Sarah Jaffe, *Work Won't Love You Back: How Devotion to Our Jobs Keeps Us Exploited, Exhausted, and Alone* (New York: Bold Type Books, 2021), 34.
    "While there have always been": Gayle Kauffman, quoted in Anne Branigin, "The January Jobs Report Wasn't Great For Women. What Could the Rest of 2022 Look Like?" *The Washington Post*, February 8, 2022, www.washingtonpost.com/lifestyle/2022/02/08/january-jobs-report-women.
    This despite the fact: Janell Fetterolf, "In Many Countries, at Least Four-in-Ten in the Labor Force Are Women," Pew Research Center, March 7, 2017, www.pewresearch.org/fact-tank/2017/03/07/in-many-countries-at-least-four-in-ten-in-the-labor-force-are-women.

21   *Women of color face*: Anu Kumar, "It's Time to Face the Facts: We Have a Gender and Diversity Problem in the Nonprofit World," *Forbes*, February 3, 2020, www.forbes.com/sites/forbesnonprofitcouncil/2020/02/03/its-time-to-face-the-facts-we-have-a-gender-and-diversity-problem-in-the-nonprofit-world.
    "Quite simply, the pool": Christina Darnell, "Christian Nonprofit CEOs Mostly White, Mostly Male," MinistryWatch, September 14, 2020, ministrywatch.com/christian-nonprofit-ceos-mostly-white-mostly-male.

22   *Women and girls have unique*: Lisa Kurbiel, "Investing in the SDGs in a post COVID world," United Nations Sustainable Development Group, January 26, 2021, unsdg.un.org/latest/blog/investing-sdgs-post-covid-world.
    The provision of sexual: Kurbiel, "Investing in the SDGs."
    The concerted effort: "Levels & Trends in Child Mortality: Report 2019," United Nations Inter-agency Group for Child Mortality Estimation, United Nations Children's Fund, 2019, www.unicef.org/media/60561/file/UN-IGME-child-mortality-report-2019.pdf.
    Before the Covid-19 pandemic: "Progress on the Sustainable Development Goals: The Gender Snapshot 2020," UN Women, 2020, www.unwomen.org/en/digital-library/publications/2020/09/progress-on-the-sustainable-development-goals-the-gender-snapshot-2020.
    Around the world: "UN Policy Brief: The Impact of Covid 19 on Women," UN Women, United Nations Department of Economic and Social Affairs, April 2020, www.un.org/sexualviolenceinconflict/wp-content/uploads/2020/06/report/policy-brief-the-impact-of-covid-19-on-women/policy-brief-the-impact-of-covid-19out-on-women-en-1.pdf.

23   *Violence against women*: "UN Policy Brief," UN Women.
    At least 200 million girls: "Female Genital Mutilation (FGM)," UNICEF, February 2020, data.unicef.org/topic/child-protection/female-genital-mutilation.
    Women have a 27 percent higher: "Progress on the Sustainable Development Goals," UN Women.
    Natural disasters are disastrous: "Progress on the Sustainable Development Goals," UN Women.

2. A CULTURE OF BELONGING

24   *Among them*: Jessica Bennet, *Feminist Fight Club: A Survival Manual for a Sexist Workplace* (New York: Harper Wave, 2016).

25   *Not long after Sarah*: Unless a person is specifically identified in this book, names and circumstances have been changed to protect anonymity.

27   *"Clear enough to set"*: Gender Practitioners Collaborative, "Minimum Standards for Mainstreaming Gender Equality," Gender Standards, accessed February 9, 2022, genderstandards.org/standards/.

28 *Wheaton Network Initiative*: "Principles," Wheaton College, copyright 2022, www
.wheaton.edu/academics/global-programs-and-studies/gaining-a-global-perspective
/network-initiative-gender-development-christianity/about-us/principles-/.

30 *"Diversity is being asked"*: Vernā Myers, "Diversity and Inclusion Training," The Vernā
Myers Company, copyright 2022, www.vernamyers.com.
"When an organization starts": Interview with Sandra Van Opstal, executive director of
Chasing Justice and author of *The Next Worship* (Downers Grove, IL: InterVarsity
Press, 2015), May 5, 2020.

31 *"They bring different, important"*: David A. Thomas and Robin J. Ely, "Making Differences Matter: A New Paradigm for Managing Diversity," *Harvard Business Review* 74,
no. 5 (1996): 79-90, hbr.org/1996/09/making-differences-matter-a-new-paradigm-for
-managing-diversity.
Deep-level diversity: Tomas Chamorro-Premuzic, "Does Diversity Actually Increase
Creativity?" *Harvard Business Review*, June 28, 2017, hbr.org/2017/06/does-diversity
-actually-increase-creativity.

33 *Learner safety*: Timothy R. Clark, *The 4 Stages of Psychological Safety: Defining the Path
to Inclusion and Innovation* (Oakland, CA: Berrett-Koehler Publishers, 2020), 45.
The four stages: Clark, *The 4 Stages*.
"Challenger safety is a level": Clark, *The 4 Stages*, 99.

34 *Safe organizations destigmatize failure*: Amy C. Edmondson, *The Fearless Organization:
Creating Psychological Safety in the Workplace for Learning, Innovation, and Growth*
(Hoboken, NJ: Wiley, 2018), 176.

35 *"When I was five"*: Interview with Renee Blanding, vice president of medical affairs at
Johns Hopkins Bayview Medical Center, assistant professor of anesthesiology and
critical care medicine, July 1, 2020.

36 *A Gallup survey*: Gallup, *State of the American Manager: Analytics and Advice for
Leaders*, Gallup, 2015, www.gallup.com/services/182138/state-american-manager
.aspx.

37 *"We'll struggle to be"*: Ashlee Eiland, *Human(kind): How Reclaiming Human Worth and
Embracing Radical Kindness Will Bring Us Back Together* (Colorado Springs: Water-
Brook, 2020), 155.

38 *This bottom-up emphasis*: Miki Tsusaka, Martin Reeves, Stephanie Hurder, and Johann
D. Harnoss, "Diversity at Work," BCG Henderson Institute, July 20, 2017, www.bcg
.com/publications/2017/diversity-at-work.

39 *Only 32 percent*: Gallup, *State of the Global Workplace*, Gallup, 2021, www.gallup
.com/workplace/349484/state-of-the-global-workplace.aspx.
An average of 60 percent: Gallup, *State of the Global Workplace*.
Top drivers of women's exit: Vivian Hunt, Sundiatu Dixon-Fyle, Sara Prince, and Kevin
Dolan, *Diversity Wins: How Inclusion Matters* (McKinsey and Co., May 2020), www
.mckinsey.com/~/media/mckinsey/featured%20insights/diversity%20and%20inclusion
/diversity%20wins%20how%20inclusion%20matters/diversity-wins-how-inclusion
-matters-vf.pdf.

41 *"A wholehearted commitment"*: Linda Mitz Sadiq, "Bringing Organizational Well-Being
to Life," Stanford Social Innovation Review, August 12, 2020, ssir.org/articles/entry
/bringing_organizational_well_being_to_life.
Millennials will make up: "The Deloitte Global 2021 Millennial and Gen Z Survey,"
Deloitte, 2021, https://www2.deloitte.com/global/en/pages/about-deloitte/articles
/millennialsurvey-2021.html.

3. *IMAGO DEI*—ADDRESSING THEOLOGY

43   *"Ancient intellectual greats"*: Christia Mercer, "The Philosophical Origins of Patriarchy: Plato, Hippocrates, and Aristotle Laid the Foundations on Which Centuries of Sexism Were Built," *The Nation*, July 1, 2019, www.thenation.com/article/archive/patriarchy-sexism-philosophy-reproductive-rights.

     "Before we were baptized": Lisa Sharon Harper, "The Very Good News for Women for Such a Time as This," [Presentation], Created to Thrive, CBE International Conference, Houston, TX, 2019.

44   *Baptism. . . . connected"*: Lisa Sharon Harper, *The Very Good Gospel: How Everything Wrong Can Be Made Right* (Colorado Springs: WaterBrook, 2020), 152.

     The word is used: "God Created Woman as an Ezer Kind of Helper (Genesis 2:18)," Theology of Work Project, accessed February 12, 2022. www.theologyofwork.org/key-topics/women-and-work-in-the-old-testament/god-created-woman-as-an-ezer-kind-of-helper-genesis-218.

     "While businesses and organizations": Mimi Haddad, "Diversity Works," *Mutuality*, Autumn 2013, www.cbeinternational.org/sites/default/files/diversity_works_haddad.pdf.

45   *"The narrative of creation"*: Stanley J. Grenz, *Created for Community: Connecting Christian Belief with Christian Living*, 2nd ed. (Grand Rapids, MI: Baker Academic, 1996), 79.

     No scriptural case: Mimi Haddad, "Women and Men Leading Together," [Workshop], Created to Thrive, CBE International Conference, Houston, TX, 2019.

46   *John MacArthur authoritatively said*: Bob Smietana, "Accusing SBC of 'Caving,' John MacArthur Says of Beth Moore: 'Go Home,'" Religion News Service, October 19, 2019, religionnews.com/2019/10/19/accusing-sbc-of-caving-john-macarthur-says-beth-moore-should-go-home.

47   *"If you strive to carve"*: John Piper, "Is There a Place for Female Professors at Seminary?" *Ask Pastor John* podcast, January 22, 2018, www.desiringgod.org/interviews/is-there-a-place-for-female-professors-at-seminary.

     During the election campaign: Yonat Shimron and Emily McFarlan Miller, "Some Southern Baptist Pastors Are Calling Kamala Harris 'Jezebel.' What Do They Mean?" Religion News Service, January 29, 2021, religionnews.com/2021/01/29/southern-baptist-pastors-are-calling-kamala-harris-jezebel-what-do-they-mean.

49   *As a collective at the Wheaton Network Initiative*: "Principles," Wheaton College, copyright 2022, www.wheaton.edu/academics/global-programs-and-studies/gaining-a-global-perspective/network-initiative-gender-development-christianity/about-us/principles-/.

50   *Wheaton Initiative statement*: Wheaton Network Initiative on Gender, Development and Christianity, "Principles for Gender Equality for Development Organizations: God's Design of Women and Men Together," accessed April 12, 2022, https://www.wheaton.edu/academics/global-programs-and-studies/gaining-a-global-perspective/network-initiative-gender-development-christianity/about-us/principles-/.

4. A CLEAR CASE

52   *"Work of diversity and inclusion"*: Presentation by Nikki Lerner at an internal staff meeting July 19, 2021; see www.nikkilerner.com.

53   *More than a quarter of employees*: Ben Wigert and Sangeeta Agrawal, "Employee Burnout, Part 1: The 5 Main Causes," Gallup, July 12, 2018, https://www.gallup.com/workplace/358349/gender-gap-worker-burnout-widened-amid-pandemic.aspx.

     Men have one primary identity: Robin J. Ely and Irene Padavic, "What's Really Holding Women Back?" *Harvard Business Review*, February 19, 2020, hbr.org/2020/03/whats-really-holding-women-back.

54   *Women and men making decisions*: Vivian Hunt, Dennis Layton, and Sara Prince, *Diversity Matters*, McKinsey & Co., February 2, 2015, www.mckinsey.com/insights/organ ization/~/media/2497d4ae4b534ee89d929cc6e3aea485.ashx.

     Studies confirm that particularly women: C. C. Perez, *Invisible Women: Data Bias in a World Designed for Men* (New York: Abrams Press, 2019), 266.

55   *An international study*: Marcus Noland, Tyler Moran, and Barbara Kotschwar, "Is Gender Diversity Profitable? Evidence from a Global Survey," *Peterson Institute for International Economics* 16, no. 3 (2016): 1-35.

     Companies in the top quartile: Vivian Hunt, Sundiatu Dixon-Fyle, Sara Prince, and Kevin Dolan, *Diversity Wins: How Inclusion Matters*, McKinsey & Co., May 2020, www.mckinsey .com/~/media/featured%20insights/diversity%20and%20inclusion/diversity%20 wins%20how%20inclusion%20matters/diversity-wins-how-inclusion-matters-vf.pdf.

56   *Companies with more than 30 percent*: Hunt et al., *Diversity Wins*. Similar results were found in relation to ethnic and cultural diversity.

     Study of S&P 500 companies: Dieter Holger, "The Business Case for More Diversity," *The Wall Street Journal*, October 26, 2019, www.wsj.com/articles/the-business-case -for-more-diversity-11572091200.

     "Different perspectives on customer needs": Vivian Hunt, Lareina Yee, Sara Prince, and Sundiatu Dixon-Fyle, "Delivering Through Diversity," McKinsey & Co., January 18, 2018, www.mckinsey.com/business-functions/organization/our-insights/delivering -through-diversity#.

     Organizations require mechanisms: Miki Tsusaka, Martin Reeves, and Johann D. Harnoss, "Diversity at Work," BCG Henderson Institute, July 20, 2017, www.bcg.com /publications/2017/diversity-at-work.

57   *The debate and unfamiliarity*: David Rock, Heidi Grant, and Jacqui Grey, "Diverse Teams Feel Less Comfortable—and That's Why They Perform Better," *Harvard Business Review*, September 22, 2016, hbr.org/2016/09/diverse-teams-feel-less -comfortable-and-thats-why-they-perform-better.

58   *Having more diversity*: Katherine W. Phillips, Katie A. Liljenquist, and Margaret A. Neale, "Is the Pain Worth the Gain? The Advantages and Liabilities of Agreeing with Socially Distinct Newcomers," *Personality and Social Psychology Bulletin* 35 (2009): 336-50, journals.sagepub.com/doi/abs/10.1177/0146167208328062.

     Goes against many people's intuitions: Rock, Grant, and Grey, "Diverse Teams Feel Less Comfortable."

59   *A study in Europe*: Cristina Díaz-García, Angela González-Moreno, and Francisco Jose Sáez-Martínez, "Gender Diversity Within R&D Teams: Its Impact on Radicalness of Innovation," *Innovation* 15, no. 2 (2013): 149-60.

60   *"But when members"*: Katherine W. Phillips, "How Diversity Makes Us Smarter: Being Around People Who Are Different from Us Makes Us More Creative, More Diligent and Harder-Working," *Scientific American*, October 1, 2014, www.scientificamerican .com/article/how-diversity-makes-us-smarter.

     It provokes more thought: Phillips, "How Diversity Makes Us Smarter."

     "See their ideas move": Sylvia Ann Hewlett, Ripa Rashid, and Laura Sherbin, "Diversity's Positive Impact on Innovation and Outcomes," *The Global Talent Competitiveness Index 2018* (Coqual, 2018), 45-51, www.talentinnovation.org/Diversity%C3%A2% E2%82%AC%E2%84%A2s-Positive-Impact-on-Innovation-and-Outcomes-CTI -Chapter.pdf.

     Diversity supports innovative thinking: Tsusaka et al., "Diversity at Work."

62   *Women are more likely to give*: Lindsay Walker, "Gender Matters: New Research
     Explores Philanthropic Giving to Women's Causes," *Nonprofit Quarterly*, June 13,
     2016, nonprofitquarterly.org/gender-matters-new-research-explores-philanthropic
     -giving-to-womens-causes.
     Gender diversity is an asset: "Gender Diversity, a Corporate Performance Driver,"
     McKinsey & Co., October 1, 2007, www.mckinsey.com/business-functions/organi
     zation/our-insights/gender-diversity-a-corporate-performance-driver.
     Coalitions are being formed: "The Women's Philanthropy Institute: Research That
     Grows Women's Philanthropy," IUPUI Women's Philanthropy Institute, Lilly Family
     School of Philanthropy, accessed February 16, 2022, philanthropy.iupui.edu/doc
     /institutes/wpi-research-overview2019.PDF.
     Supreme Court Justice: Ruth Bader Ginsburg, as quoted in Jill Filipovic, "Justice Gins-
     burg's Distant Dream of an All-Female Supreme Court," *The Guardian*, November 30,
     2012, www.theguardian.com/commentisfree/2012/nov/30/justice-ginsburg-all
     -female-supreme-court.

63   *A minimum of 30 percent*: Marcus Noland, Tyler Moran, and Barbara Kotschwar, "Is
     Gender Diversity Profitable? Evidence from a Global Survey," Working Paper
     Series, Peterson Institute for International Economics, February 2016, www.piie
     .com/publications/working-papers/gender-diversity-profitable-evidence-global
     -survey.

5. A RECLAIMED ORGANIZATIONAL CULTURE

64   *81 percent of women*: "2018 Study on Sexual Harassment and Assault," Stop Street Ha-
     rassment, February 21, 2018, stopstreetharassment.org/our-work/nationalstudy
     /2018-national-sexual-abuse-report.

65   *Thirty-eight percent of women*: "2018 Study on Sexual Harassment and Assault," Stop
     Street Harassment.
     One in six employees of churches: "Sexual Harassment in the Christian Workplace: Ex-
     ecutive Report 2020," Church Law & Tax Store, *Christianity Today*, 2020, store
     .churchlawandtax.com/sexual-harassment-in-the-christian-workplace-executive
     -report-2020.
     It's also noteworthy: "Sexual Harassment in the Christian Workplace," Church Law and
     Tax Store.
     "Far more hesitant": "Working Relationships in the #MeToo Era: Key Findings," Lean
     In, 2019, leanin.org/sexual-harassment-backlash-survey-results.

66   *Techniques churches have used*: Scot McKnight and Laura Barringer, *A Church Called
     Tov: Forming a Goodness Culture that Resists Abuses of Power and Promotes Healing*
     (Carol Stream, IL: Tyndale Momentum, 2020).

67   *"Sexual harassment is not about sex"*: Gretchen Carlson, "How We Can End Sexual Ha-
     rassment at Work," TED, October 2017, www.ted.com/talks/gretchen_carlson
     _how_we_can_end_sexual_harassment_at_work.
     In a well-documented incident: "Sexual Exploitation and Abuse in the Aid Sector," House
     of Commons, UK Parliament, July 2018, publications.parliament.uk/pa/cm201719
     /cmselect/cmintdev/840/84002.htm.

68   *"Catastrophic failure of protection"*: Inter-Agency Standing Committee Task Force on
     Protection from Sexual Exploitation and Abuse, "Sexual Exploitation and Abuse by
     UN, NGO and INGO Personnel: A Self-Assessment," Humanitarian Practice Network,

June 2012, https://odihpn.org/publication/sexual-exploitation-and-abuse-by-un
-ngo-and-ingo-personnel-a-self-assessment/.

"Head offices had not given": Inter-Agency Standing Committee Task Force, "Sexual Exploitation and Abuse."

69   *The effects of sexual harassment*: Holly Kearl, *50 Stories About Stopping Street Harassers* (Marston Gate: Amazon, 2013).

"The body can experience": Nicole Spector, "The Hidden Health Effects of Sexual Harassment," NBC News, October 13, 2017, www.nbcnews.com/better/health/hidden -health-effects-sexual-harassment-ncna810416.

"A seemingly small assault": Elizabeth Hopper, "What Is a Microaggression? Everyday Insults with Harmful Effects," Thought Co., July 3, 2019, www.thoughtco.com /microaggression-definition-examples-4171853.

Microaggressions are also characterized: Hopper, "What Is a Microaggression?"

70   *An entire day's worth of microaggressions*: Austin Channing Brown, *I'm Still Here: Black Dignity in a World Made for Whiteness* (New York: Convergent Books, 2018).

"In my early days": Jeanne Porter King, "Breaking Down Barriers for Women in Church Leadership," in *Created to Thrive*, ed. Elizabeth Beyer (Minneapolis: CBE International, 2021), 162-72.

71   *This is an example*: P. Johnson, "Sexism," *Encyclopedia of Applied Ethics*, 2nd ed., ed. Ruth Chadwick (New York: Academic Press, 2012), 84-90.

73   *Increasing the representation of women*: Marianne Cooper, "The Power of Us: How We Stop Sexual Harassment," TED, January 2018, www.ted.com/talks/marianne_cooper _the_power_of_us_how_we_stop_sexual_harassment.

"The single biggest predictor": Marianne Cooper, "The 3 Things That Make Organizations More Prone to Sexual Harassment," *The Atlantic*, November 27, 2017, www.the atlantic.com/business/archive/2017/11/organizations-sexual-harassment/546707.

Cracking down on harassers: Cooper, "The 3 Things."

"Managers play a central role": "Women in the Workplace 2019," Lean In, 2019, leanin. org/women-in-the-workplace-report-2019.

74   *"They were designed"*: Michelle King, "It's Not You, It's Your Workplace," TED, June 2019, www.ted.com/talks/michelle_king_it_s_not_you_it_s_your_workplace.

75   *"56 percent of American workers"*: Mary Abbajay, "What to Do When You Have a Bad Boss," *Harvard Business Review*, September 7, 2018, hbr.org/2018/09/what-to-do -when-you-have-a-bad-boss.

Myriad books, podcasts, and articles: See, for example, Mike Cosper, "Who Killed Mars Hill?" *The Rise and Fall of Mars Hill*, podcast, episode 1, June 21, 2021, Christianity Today, www.christianitytoday.com/ct/podcasts/rise-and-fall-of-mars-hill; Kristen Kobes Du Mez, *Jesus and John Wayne: How White Evangelicals Corrupted a Faith and Fractured a Nation* (New York: Liveright, 2020).

Trump was supported: Jack Jenkins, "Study: Trump Expanded Evangelical Support in 2020, but Biden Gained with Other White Christians," Religion News, July 2, 2021, religionnews.com/2021/07/02/study-trump-expanded-evangelical-support-in -2020-but-biden-gained-with-other-white-christians.

76   *At one end*: Jonathan H. Westover, "How Much Are Toxic Leaders Costing Your Business?" *Forbes*, May 27, 2020, www.forbes.com/sites/forbescoaches council/2020/05/27/how-much-are-toxic-leaders-costing-your-business.

"Kissing up and kicking down": Yvonne Brown, "How Toxic Leaders Damage Your Business and What to Do About It," *Forbes*, August 8, 2016, www.forbes.com/sites

/forbescoachescouncil/2016/08/08/how-toxic-leaders-damage-your-business
-and-what-to-do-about-it.

"Leaders, even bad leaders": Barbara Kellerman, *Bad Leadership: What It Is, How It Happens and Why It Matters* (Boston: Harvard University Press, 2005).

77 *People's tendency to be seduced*: Tomas Chamorro-Premuzic, *Why Do so Many Incompetent Men Become Leaders? (And How to Fix It)* (Boston: Harvard Business Review Press, 2019).

Feminine qualities surfaced: Michael D'Antonio and John Gerzema, *The Athena Doctrine: How Women (and the Men Who Think Like Them) Will Rule the Future* (San Francisco: Jossey-Bass, 2013).

The ways masculine and feminine: We speak here in the binary male/female. We acknowledge this is an oversimplification of terminology and reality in our present-day context.

78 *"Conventional wisdom on the gender gap"*: Marissa Orr, *Lean Out: The Truth About Women, Power, and the Workplace* (New York: HarperCollins Leadership, 2019), 101. *"Diversity doesn't happen"*: Orr, *Lean Out*, 139.

79 *Eighty-five percent of women*: Bourree Lam, "How Office Culture Can Crush Women's Ambitions," *The Atlantic*, April 20, 2017, www.theatlantic.com/business/archive/2017/04/ambition-office-women/523443/.

81 *"Debates over superiority"*: Carolyn Custis James, *When Life and Beliefs Collide: How Knowing God Makes a Difference* (Grand Rapids, MI: Zondervan, 2003).

Scripture offers us a model: Aimee Byrd, *Why Can't We Be Friends? Avoidance Is Not Purity* (Phillipsburg, NJ: P&R Publishing, 2018), 113.

Drawing on the social meaning: Byrd, *Why Can't We Be Friends?*, 114-115.

"God's people ought": Joseph Hellerman, *The Ancient Church as a Family* (Minneapolis: Fortress Press, 2001), as quoted by Byrd, *Why Can't We Be Friends?*, 115.

6. HUMAN RESOURCES FOR CULTURES OF BELONGING

84 *Gender alone does not explain*: "Women in the Workplace 2018," Lean In, McKinsey & Company, 2018, womenintheworkplace.com/2018.

86 *Male- or female-gendered wording*: Danielle Gaucher, Justin Friesen, and Aaron C. Kay, "Evidence That Gendered Wording in Job Advertisements Exists and Sustains Gender Inequality," *Journal of Personality and Social Psychology* 101, no. 1 (2011): 109-28.

Terms like "ambitious": Emily Peck, "Here Are the Words That May Keep Women from Applying for Jobs," HuffPost, December 7, 2017, www.huffpost.com/entry/textio-unitive-bias-software_n_7493624.

Removing gender and cultural identifiers: Tristan L. Botelho and Mabel Abraham, "Research: Objective Performance Metrics are Not Enough to Overcome Gender Bias," *Harvard Business Review*, October 25, 2017, hbr.org/2017/10/research-objective-performance-metrics-are-not-enough-to-overcome-gender-bias.

87 *A blind review of résumés*: Rebecca Knight, "7 Practical Ways to Reduce Bias in Your Hiring Process," *Harvard Business Review*, June 12, 2017, hbr.org/2017/06/7-practical-ways-to-reduce-bias-in-your-hiring-process.

A study on hiring as cultural: Lauren A. Rivera, "Hiring as Cultural Matching," *American Sociological Review* 77, no. 6 (2012): 999-1022.

Concerns about absolute productivity: Rivera, "Hiring as Cultural Matching."

Predetermined interview questions: "Structured Interviews: Four Key Advantages to Using Them," Corvirtus, January 29, 2021, corvirtus.com/four-key-advantages-to-using-structured-interviews.

89 *It takes a project-based approach*: "Women in the Workplace: Why Women Make Great Leaders & How to Retain Them," Center for Creative Leadership, December 2, 2019, www.ccl.org/articles/white-papers/7-reasons-want-women-workplace.

90 *Self-evaluation and self-rating*: Gardiner Morse, "Designing a Bias-Free Organization," *Harvard Business Review*, August 24, 2016, hbr.org/2016/07/designing-a-bias-free-organization.
   Women specifically benefit: Paola Cecchi-Dimeglio, "How Gender Bias Corrupts Performance Reviews, and What to Do About It," *Harvard Business Review*, April 12, 2017, hbr.org/2017/04/how-gender-bias-corrupts-performance-reviews-and-what-to-do-about-it.

91 *Perceptions still trump reality*: Tomas Chamorro-Premuzic, "As Long as We Associate Leadership with Masculinity, Women Will Be Overlooked," *Harvard Business Review*, March 8, 2019, hbr.org/2019/03/as-long-as-we-associate-leadership-with-masculinity-women-will-be-overlooked.

92 *Progress at the top is constrained*: "Women in the Workplace 2019," McKinsey & Co., Lean In, 2019, womenintheworkplace.com/2019.

93 *There are simply too few women*: "Women in the Workplace 2019," McKinsey & Co., Lean In.
   "Entry-level women": Sandrine Devillard, Vivian Hunt, and Larina Yee, "Still Looking for Room at the Top: Ten Years of Research on Women in the Workplace," *McKinsey Quarterly*, March 8, 2018, www.mckinsey.com/featured-insights/gender-equality/still-looking-for-room-at-the-top-ten-years-of-research-on-women-in-the-workplace.

94 *Simple steps to improve*: Rob Gray, "Why You Need to Ditch the Nine Box Grid," *HR Magazine*, February 24, 2016, www.hrmagazine.co.uk/content/features/why-you-need-to-ditch-the-nine-box-grid; Deb Calvert, "Behind the Scenes: How a 9-Box Talent Review Model May Hurt You Professionally," People First Productivity Solutions, Medium, January 19, 2017, peoplefirstps.medium.com/behind-the-scenes-how-a-9-box-talent-review-model-may-hurt-you-professionally-9c4d113f05bd.
   The majority of workers don't want: Aaron DeSmet, Bonnie Dowling, Mihir Mysore, and Angelika Reich, "It's Time for Leaders to Get Real About Hybrid," *McKinsey Quarterly*, July 9, 2021, www.mckinsey.com/business-functions/organization/our-insights/its-time-for-leaders-to-get-real-about-hybrid.

96 *In this stage*: Courtney Hesselbacher and Bailey Nelson, "Sustain a Work Culture that Works for New Moms," Gallup, May 14, 2019, www.gallup.com/workplace/257504/sustain-work-culture-works-new-moms.aspx.

7. DEVELOPING PEOPLE FOR CULTURES OF BELONGING

104 *Since the #MeToo movement*: Tim Bower, "The #MeToo Backlash," *Harvard Business Review*, September–October 2019, hbr.org/2019/09/the-metoo-backlash.

105 *A useful framework*: Belinda Bauman, *Brave Souls: Experiencing the Audacious Power of Empathy* (Downers Grove, IL: InterVarsity Press, 2019).
   "The way of empathy": Bauman, *Brave Souls*, 51.
   Efforts to be a better listener: Interview with Craig Stewart, CEO, The Warehouse Trust, Cape Town, South Africa, June 29, 2020.

106   *"The mismatch between qualities"*: Robin J. Ely, Herminia Ibarra, and Deborah M. Kolb, "Taking Gender into Account: Theory and Design for Women's Leadership Development Programs," *Academy of Management Learning & Education* 10, no. 3 (September 2011).

108   *Poverty as a consequence*: Bryant L. Myers, *Walking with the Poor: Principles and Practices of Transformational Development* (Maryknoll, NY: Orbis Books, 2014).

109   *Leadership traits displayed by women*: Natacha Catalino and Kirstan Marnane, "When Women Lead, Workplaces Should Listen," *McKinsey Quarterly*, December 11, 2019, www.mckinsey.com/featured-insights/leadership/when-women-lead-work places-should-listen.

111   *"Women get less frequent"*: Catherine H. Tinsley and Robin J. Ely, "What Most Companies Get Wrong About Men and Women," *Harvard Business Review,* April 17, 2018, hbr .org/2018/05/what-most-people-get-wrong-about-men-and-women.
        "The mentor goes beyond giving feedback": Herminia Ibarra, Nancy M. Carter, and Christine Silva, "Why Men Still Get More Promotions Than Women," *Harvard Business Review,* September 7, 2010, hbr.org/2010/09/why-men-still-get-more -promotions-than-women.

112   *People are less embedded*: Tinsley and Ely, "What Most Companies Get Wrong."
        "Without sponsorship": Ibarra, Carter, and Silva, "Why Men Still Get More Promotions Than Women."
        "Finding a sponsor at the top": Nancy M. Carter and Christine Silva, "Mentoring: Necessary but Insufficient for Advancement," Catalyst, 2010, www.catalyst.org/wp-content /uploads/2019/01/Mentoring_Necessary_But_Insufficient_for_Advancement_Final _120610.pdf.

8. THE LEADERSHIP WILL TO MAKE A CHANGE

120   *Leadership will*: Vivian Hunt, Sara Prince, Sundiatu Dixon-Fyle, and Lareina Yee, "De-livering Through Diversity," McKinsey and Company, January 2018, https://www .mckinsey.com/business-functions/people-and-organizational-performance/our -insights/delivering-through-diversity.
        "Strong, visible, active leadership": "Gender Equality and Women's Voice," CARE International, February 2018, https://insights.careinternational.org.uk/publications /gender-equality-and-women-s-voice-guidance-note.
        Millennials are 25 percent more likely: Dan Schawbel, "Are Millennials Putting an End to Gender Differences?" *Newsweek*, November 18, 2017, www.newsweek.com/are -millennials-putting-end-gender-differences-715922.

121   *"Tend to become"*: Michelle Travis, "How and Why Dads of Daughters Are Leaders in Women's Advancement," The Way Women Work, accessed April 3, 2022, https:// thewaywomenwork.com/2019/11/how-and-why-dads-of-daughters-are-leaders -in-womens-advancement.
        "Are we fighting poverty": Interview with Craig Stewart, CEO of The Warehouse Trust, Cape Town, South Africa, June 29, 2020.
        "It's not enough that men": Interview with Prabu Deepan, head of thematic support at TearFund UK, previously global gender and protection unit lead, June 24, 2020.

123   *"When privileged people are required"*: Christena Cleveland, "How Can Privileged Christians Work Strategically for Equality?" YouTube, May 21, 2017, youtu.be/tJlt1zwGZqM.

125   *"As a young man"*: Interview with Deepan.

131   *donors rarely ask questions about diversity*: Vivian Hunt, Sundiatu Dixon-Fyle, Sara Prince, and Kevin Dolan, *Diversity Wins: How Inclusion Matters*, McKinsey & Co., May 2020, https://www.mckinsey.com/~/media/mckinsey/featured%20insights

/diversity%20and%20inclusion/diversity%20wins%20how%20inclusion%20
matters/diversity-wins-how-inclusion-matters-vf.pdf.

"The problem of toxic masculinity": Interview with Stewart.

132 *The familiar story of the bleeding woman*: Cleveland, "How Can Privileged Christians
Work Strategically for Equality?"

9. WOMEN AND MEN BEYOND THE WORKPLACE

134 *"How much longer"*: C. Nicole Mason, "I Felt like I Had to Go Part-Time When My Kids
Were Young. This Shouldn't Be the Norm," The Lily, July 9, 2020, https://www.thelily
.com/i-felt-like-i-had-to-go-part-time-when-my-kids-were-young-this-shouldnt-be
-the-norm/.

Nearly 3 million women: Megan Cerullo, "Nearly 3 Million U.S. Women Have Dropped
out of the Labor Force in the Past Year," CBS News, February 5, 2021, www.cbsnews
.com/news/covid-crisis-3-million-women-labor-force.

Women's employment fell: "Policy Brief: Building Forward Fairer: Women's Rights to
Work and at Work at the Core of the COVID-19 Recovery," International Labour
Organization, July 2021, www.ilo.org/wcmsp5/groups/public/---dgreports/---gender
/documents/publication/wcms_814499.pdf.

135 *Female-dominated sectors*: Johnny Wood, "COVID-19 Has Worsened Gender Inequality. These Charts Show What We Can Do About It," World Economic Forum,
September 4, 2020, www.weforum.org/agenda/2020/09/covid-19-gender-inequality
-jobs-economy.

"Other countries have social": Anne Helen Petersen, "Other Countries Have Social
Safety Nets. The U.S. Has Women," Culture Study, November 11, 2020, annehelen
.substack.com/p/other-countries-have-social-safety.

The monetary value: Gus Wezerek and Kristen R. Ghodsee, "Women's Unpaid Labor Is
Worth $10,900,000,000,000," Opinion, *New York Times*, March 5, 2020, www
.nytimes.com/interactive/2020/03/04/opinion/women-unpaid-labor.html.

$88 trillion global economy: Iman Ghosh, "The $88 Trillion World Economy in One
Chart," Visual Capitalist, September 14, 2020, www.visualcapitalist.com/the-88
-trillion-world-economy-in-one-chart.

The free labor of women: "Calculating the Value of Women's Unpaid Work," The FRED
Blog, March 9, 2020, fredblog.stlouisfed.org/2020/03/calculating-the-value-of
-womens-unpaid-work.

136 *"Everyone acknowledges"*: C. C. Perez, *Invisible Women: Data Bias in a World Designed
for Men* (New York: Abrams Press, 2019), 240-41.

Men's free labor consists: Abigail Johnson Hess, "Here's How Much More Women Could
Earn if Household Chores Were Compensated," CNBC Make It, April 11, 2018, www
.cnbc.com/2018/04/10/heres-what-women-could-earn-if-household-chores-were
-compensated.html.

137 *Women overall earn 82 cents*: Katharina Buchholz, "Gender Pay Gap: Women Earn
Nearly 20% Less Than Their Male Counterparts, Study Shows," World Economic
Forum, October 28, 2021, www.weforum.org/agenda/2021/10/the-gender-pay
-gap-visualized.

Women's employment continues: Janell Fetterolf, "In Many Countries, at Least Four-in-
Ten in the Labor Force are Women," Pew Research Center, March 7, 2017, www.pew
research.org/fact-tank/2017/03/07/in-many-countries-at-least-four-in-ten-in-the
-labor-force-are-women.

139   *She would tiptoe out*: Sheryl Sandberg, *Lean In: Women, Work, and the Will to Lead* (New York, Knopf, 2013), 128.

140   *And if it's made by humans*: This notion borrowed from Glennon Doyle, *Untamed* (New York: The Dial Press, 2020).
"It is not about": Gregg McKeown, *Essentialism: The Disciplined Pursuit of Less* (New York: Currency Publishing, 2014).

141   *Christina describes designing a space for herself*: Interview with Christina Klinepeter, executive and Team USA Karate Athlete, June 19, 2020.

142   *"My parents are first-generation"*: Interview with Jenny Yang, SVP of advocacy for World Relief, coauthor with Matthew Soerens of *Welcoming the Stranger: Justice, Compassion & Truth in the Immigration Debate* (Downers Grove, IL: InterVarsity Press, 2009), June 10, 2020.

143   *People who are ambitious*: Timothy A. Judge and John D. Kammeyer-Mueller, "On the Value of Aiming High: The Causes and Consequences of Ambition," *Journal of Applied Psychology* 97, no. 4 (2012): 758-75.

144   *"There is a cultural narrative"*: Interview with Amy McCullough, lead pastor at Grace United Methodist Church Baltimore, author of *Her Preaching Body: Conversations About Identity, Agency, and Embodiment Among Contemporary Female Preachers* (Eugene, OR: Cascade, 2018), June 4, 2020.

146   *The third space theory*: First introduced by Homi K. Bhabha, *The Location of Culture* (London: Routledge, 1994), 55.
"As a lens by citizens": Elina Henttonen and Kirsi LaPointe, *Työelämän Toisinajattelijat* (Helsinki: Gaudeamus, 2015), ebook, author's translation.
By Muslim women from conservative backgrounds: Golnaz Golnaraghi and Sumayya Daghar, "Feminism in the Third Space—Critical Discourse Analysis of Mipsterz Women and Grassroots Activism," Emerald, April 11, 2017, www.emerald.com /insight/content/doi/10.1108/S2046-607220160000003010/full/html.
"We loved our jobs": Elina Henttonen and Kirsi LaPointe, *Työelämän Toisinajattelijat*.

147   *"Incorporate people's perspectives"*: David A. Thomas and Robin J. Ely, "Making Differences Matter: A New Paradigm for Managing Diversity," *Harvard Business Review,* September–October 1996, hbr.org/1996/09/making-differences-matter-a-new -paradigm-for-managing-diversity.

148   *Google's Project Aristotle*: Michael Lee and Koen Veltman, "The Great Covid-Driven Teamwork Divide," INSEAD, October 15 2020, knowledge.insead.edu/blog/insead -blog/the-great-covid-driven-teamwork-divide-15391.
"Hard skills and expertise": Arianna Huffington, "The New Hybrid Work Model Will Require Hybrid Skills," LinkedIn, April 3, 2021, www.linkedin.com/pulse/new -hybrid-work-model-require-skills-arianna-huffington.

149   *I was an established executive*: Interview with Sachin Louis, June 5, 2020.

150   *I was raised in a home*: Interview with Dan Rickett, June 25, 2020.

151   *I came to understand*: Interview with Harold Overstreet, June 11, 2020.

154   *Michele is a facilitator*: interview with Michele Breene, August 14, 2020.

CONCLUSION

160   *"It is in the knowledge"*: Simone de Beauvoir, *The Ethics of Ambiguity*, trans. Bernard Frechtman (New York: Kensington Publishing, 1948), 9.
Her family's return to Rwanda: Interview with Sharon Greene, April 26, 2020.

ABOUT THE AUTHORS

Beth Birmingham is a founding partner in BE Development Partners, a leadership and research consulting practice currently serving as a full time consultant to Tearfund USA on the Christian Alliance for Inclusive Development. This organization serves as a status quo disrupting network for women and male allies serving in the global development sector. She has served the NGO sector the last twenty years through developing leaders as a full-time professor at Eastern University. She holds a PhD in leadership and change and an MBA in international economic development. She is a past board member of the Accord Network and is currently a member of the Wheaton Network Initiative on Development, Gender, and Christianity. She lives outside Philadelphia, Pennsylvania.

Eeva Sallinen Simard currently directs an international health project at World Relief and has more than fifteen years of experience working in management roles at nonprofits. Eeva holds an MSc in international politics from the University of Helsinki and an MBA from John Hopkins University. She is a co-convener of the Wheaton Network Initiative on Development, Gender, and Christianity. She lives in the city of Baltimore with her husband, Rene, and children Tuomas and Amelie.